"'You are not alone.' These are the four most powerful words a mom can hear. You'll 'hear' these words on the pages of this book as Becky dives into the absurd platitudes we sometimes offer one another and digs just a little deeper to find the nuggets of truth we really do need to hear."
—Jill Savage, author of *No More Perfect Moms* and founder of Hearts at Home

"As a mom of four, I've read a lot of 'mothering' books. Not like this one. Becky Baudouin cuts right through the platitudes so glibly offered to one another to offer real hope and encouragement. By authentically revealing her own stories of mothering moments gone awry, she gives the reader permission to do the same. So wish this book was available to me for those long days and short years! I will be passing this book around to the many young moms in my circle. No disclaimers needed; this book is solidly sound. Beautifully written, full of wisdom, easy to read. Bravo Becky!"
—Letitia Suk, author of *100 Need to Know Tips for Moms of Tweens and Teens*

"In *Enjoy Every Minute*, Becky Baudouin openly and honestly shares both the triumphs and the struggles of her motherhood journey. You find yourself drawn in and you don't want to put the book down. As a mother, you will find that you resonate with so many of the feelings and experiences Becky shares. I appreciate Becky's vulnerability as she writes, 'But maybe, if we had a realistic view of this motherhood journey going into it, we wouldn't beat ourselves up because we are finding some aspects of it to be harder than we ever imagined . . . . Maybe we could lock eyes with another mom and know that we could be honest, because maybe—just maybe—she is struggling, too.' It's a refreshing and encouraging read and it makes you want to extend more grace to yourself, to your children, and to those around you. I highly recommend *Enjoy Every Minute* to every Mom out there!"
—Amy Robnik Joob, mom of two, ⸺⸺⸺⸺⸺ of *Model Behavior: Make Your Career Path Your (*

"Becky is such an authentic voice in a world that sometimes feels staged and Instagram perfect. She busts mom myths by being real and sharing her struggles along with strategies to overcome them. I love how she weaves God's Word throughout the pages in such a powerful way. I feel lighter after throwing off some unrealistic expectations AND I still feel motivated and equipped to do my best as a mom and wife."

—Liz Lassa, mom of three, speaker, and creator of the *Spiritual Circle Journal*

"I LOVE this book! Becky has such a clever, fresh way of expressing herself in writing and uses great analogies to help people understand what she is saying. I also love her sense of humor with everything. It's so much easier to hear life lessons when the person helping us seems just as flawed as ourselves! She is vulnerable, willing to laugh at herself, wise, and discerning. I truly believe that any mother who reads this book will be uplifted and encouraged as they go through the parenting years. There is something for every reader."

—Tori L., mom, stepmom, and soon-to-be grandma

"For new mothers or mothers of young children, teens, or adult children, *Enjoy Every Minute* offers two beautiful gifts: grace and truth. Through stories that have us laughing out loud one minute and in tender tears the next, we are reminded that by holding on to God's hand, promises, and Word during those joyful and gut-wrenching times of motherhood, we are fully seen, affirmed, and unconditionally loved."

—Colleen H., mom to two young adult daughters

"For anyone who has too much to handle at home and feels like she is doing it all wrong, you've found your book. This is chock full of encouraging reminders, Becky's own honest shortcomings, funny anecdotes, and beautiful wisdom that ultimately point us to Christ, the One who can truly help us. I think what was most helpful to me was her transparency about her own issues; it made me feel like I am not alone. This is a celebration of family! *Enjoy Every Minute* made me laugh and cry and left me feeling hopeful."

—Steph B., mom of five adopted children

"This book is both insightful and inspiring. I really appreciate Becky's way of intertwining biblical wisdom with everyday words of advice from an experienced mom. She has something to say to moms of children of all ages and shows us how important it is to have a community. I love how this book brings to life many of the everyday struggles we all battle and reminds us that we are never alone."
—Marla B., mom of three teens and young adults

"Becky's book is a soul-watering conversation between friends. A reminder that you're not alone, the humor, hindsight, and hope will call up new stores of energy for what lies ahead. Read it for yourself, and gift it to others; we all need these words countering our inner dialogue."
—Kay S., mom of three teens, teacher, and editor

"I wish I had this book when I was a new mom! It is so encouraging— filled with relatable stories from various moms, Becky's own journey through motherhood, and applicable wisdom from the Word of God. Becky strikes the perfect balance of encouraging friend and experienced guide. She doesn't pretend to have motherhood entirely figured out, but she has developed a faith that shapes every aspect of her life, and as a result informs how she makes choices for herself and for her family. I will be gifting this to all the moms in my life, because reading it truly felt like spending time with a friend. I want everyone to have the kind of support, encouragement, and wisdom that Becky has poured into this book!"
—Tricia Clarke, makeup artist, mom to Jack, and podcast host

"Not your typical 'motherhood how-to' book. *Enjoy Every Minute* is a warm blanket of honesty and grace for a mother's journey. Becky writes as if these words are a journal entry to a trusted friend. She opens her heart and allows you to dive in to your own. Encouraging, healing, forgiving, and inspiring. I 'enjoyed every minute' while reading this book."
—Amy W., wife, mother and shuttle service driver of three boys, traveler, and collector of memories

"Beautifully written from a life honestly lived, Becky captures the practical and spiritual pilgrimage of motherhood. Her 'strength to strength' is deeply grounded in God's word, and I fully believe her words will mark the life of everyone who reads this book."
—Margie M., fellow pilgrim and blessed mom of two

"I absolutely love this book! I hope every mom gets the chance to read it. Becky helps us see how flawed some of our ideas about motherhood are and teaches us, with biblical wisdom, a much better way to think about things."
—Tina Haisman, mom of two, life coach, podcast host, and speaker

"I am so incredibly thankful for this book. It brings tears of relief and joy to my eyes, and happiness and comfort to my soul. I am encouraged to keep going as I read each and every paragraph, and it is a gift to be drawn closer to God through the gentle reminders she gives throughout these stories. Set down your to-do list and enjoy a safe space to be honest in feeling joy, frustration, vulnerability, sadness, hope, encouragement, and true victory in Christ!"
—Carolyn M., stay-at-home mom of two

"This book pulled me in right from the start! I felt as if I was reading stories out of my own life. Stories sprinkled with faith, hope, and reassurance. Becky's authenticity makes her relatable and admirable as she shares her journey in the pilgrimage of motherhood, reminding us that we are not alone. As I flipped through the pages, I was reminded of God's design for motherhood and how He is ever-present through each stage, so long as we stay connected to Him."
—Shannon K., mom of four children

"*Enjoy Every Moment* is a welcomed release of judgment. I needed the freedom that was beautifully exemplified through the pages of this book. Becky's personal stories, examples from other moms, and biblical reminders are a breath of fresh air! Thank you, Becky, for writing a book that all Mommas in different seasons can enjoy and learn from. It's genius, heart-felt and fun!"
—Danielle H., aspiring author, teacher, speaker, wife, mom, daughter of the King!

ENJOY *every* MINUTE

and other ridiculous things
we say to moms

Becky Baudouin

ISBN: 9798666598108

To the moms who inspire me, help me be brave,
and remind me of what is true.

To my mother, mother-in-law, and grandmothers for
teaching me that motherhood is a holy calling.

To the moms who have allowed me
to share their stories in this book.

To the moms who will read these pages and, hopefully,
find that they are not alone.

"With admiration for the greatness of what you
are building, when only God sees."
—Nicole Johnson, *The Invisible Woman*

Contents

Foreword

We've known Becky for about two decades. Over the years, we have been able to closely observe the way she has raised her kids and interacted with her husband, Bernie. Here are some things we know to be true of Becky: She is kind. She cries behind closed doors after giving her children a punishment they don't like. She can beautifully express how much she loves people in words, and notes from her are tucked away and saved for years. She is the hardest worker in the greater Chicagoland area (at the very least), pursuing her writing career while working as a manager at a local business and juggling three strong-willed daughters. She is the world's best cook, period. She loves her family, as is evident by the volume at which she speaks to them through the phone. She is an amazing host. Anyone can walk into Becky's house knowing they have a spot at the table, and over the years, they have. We once witnessed her spill an entire pot of beef stroganoff all over her kitchen floor (think Kevin's chili scene from *The Office*). She then went to her room and sobbed. She is "Mom" to not only her daughters but friends they bring home, too.

She is always striving to be the best mother, wife, daughter, sister, friend, coworker, and overall human that she can. She has a lively sense of humor, the perfect combination of witty and goofy. She has several accents in her repertoire, and it's even funnier when she tries the ones that aren't. She is gorgeous. She has seafoam green eyes, and her husband always says she gets prettier with age. She loves to play Toon Blast. She is great at analogies, a skill which has lent itself well in her writing and speaking careers. She has a crush on Jimmy Fallon. She would never leave her husband for him, but she might hesitate before answering if asked. She is her daughters' biggest cheerleader and has recently become a high school softball mom, a role she is embracing fully.

Becky is intelligent but willing to admit when she is wrong. She doesn't shy away from difficult conversations. She is brave. Not only has she overcome fears in her life, but she has turned around and done the exact things that scared her most as part of her career. She has accomplished a lot but maintains a humble spirit. When she accomplishes a dream, she finds another one. While their marriage is far from perfect, she and Bernie have pushed through the worst phases to get to the good. They have been transparent enough with their daughters to show them the reality of marriage while at the same time modeling the resilience that goes into loving someone for your whole life. They have also taken that message and used it to help countless other couples in their journeys.

She has had this book on her mind for years, and we are so proud of her for making it happen. She has years of parent-teacher conferences, birthdays, sex talks, dance recitals, kitchen disasters, and loads of laundry under her belt. After all of this, we think she might have a couple of worthwhile things to say. She has a unique way of thinking about and looking at the world around her, which will undoubtedly benefit whoever reads this book. She is equally honest about her parenting successes and pitfalls and values learning as she goes. She is a beautiful person and mother—we would know because we are her daughters. She continues to be one of the closest people to all three of us, whether we're away at college or still at home. She has majorly shaped who we are and who we are becoming. This is what God has called her to do, and we are so proud of her for saying yes.

We love you, Ma.

Kate (21), Claire (19), and Brenna (15) Baudouin

Glossary of Terms [1]

cli·ché, *noun*

A phrase or opinion that is overused and betrays a lack of original thought.

myth, *noun*

A widely held but false belief or idea.

plat·i·tude, *noun*

A remark or statement, especially one with a moral content, that has been used too often to be interesting or thoughtful.

ri·dic·u·lous, *adjective*

Deserving or inviting derision or mockery; absurd.

say·ing, *noun*

A short, pithy expression that generally contains advice or wisdom.

pith·y, *adjective*

(of language or style) concise and forcefully expressive.

Introduction

Before I became a mother, I had many opinions and ideas about how I would parent my children someday, as well as the expected results my extraordinary parenting would yield (which now I know were completely unrealistic). For example, I knew I would never count to three to coerce my children to obey. Children should just do what they are told the first time you tell them—no questions asked. Also, my children would be really good eaters; after all, if you feed them a variety of healthy, normal foods from the time they start eating, they will love to eat a variety of healthy, normal foods for the rest of their lives! And, my children would always be respectful. If you model respectful behavior and teach them good manners, children should never engage in rude or disrespectful behavior.

Of course, parenthood has surprised me in many ways. The counting practice I've most often needed to implement is not on my children, but rather on myself: count to ten when you get angry. One of my daughters has always been a very picky eater, even though I made my own baby food and introduced all kinds of fruits and vegetables early on. She likes to say she has a "refined palate." She can tell if, in a pinch, I purchase milk from somewhere other than our regular supplier (even when I transfer the milk into one of our regular-brand containers), and growing up, her "variety" of healthy, normal foods was not all that varied or healthy. And the temperamental teenage years have felt at times like round two of the tantrum-laden preschool years. I'm reminded all over again that I don't have control over very much in this process. Turns out, being a mom is not the tidy, predictable experience I thought it would be, and reading parenting books while I was pregnant did not equip me for even a fraction of the joys and challenges I have encountered as a mom.

Just as some of my ideas about parenting proved to be inaccurate, unhelpful, and down-right ridiculous, some of the parenting platitudes we offer one another fall short of encouraging. "Enjoy every minute" and "stay balanced" can feel like impossible endeavors and provoke guilt-ridden, negative self-talk. *Why am I not enjoying this motherhood gig more? Why do I so often feel overwhelmed and out of balance? People keep telling me to enjoy every moment, but my kids are driving me crazy! What is wrong with me?*

Good parenting is not a simple formula that yields a guaranteed outcome. It is a process of trials and errors, with lots of trials and lots of errors. It's a bit like learning to cook. You know what kind of food you like and want to make, so you watch other people do it and look for recipes that sound delicious and doable. You make your shopping list, purchase your supplies, do the prep work, and then at some point, even though you don't feel like you are ready, you have to start cooking. Sometimes everything comes together beautifully, and you can't believe you actually made something that tastes so good; other times it's a total disaster, like the time I used Cheetos as a breading for chicken. (The recipe called for cheese crackers which I did not have, so I improvised. Trial and error.) So, you make adjustments, keep on learning, and try again.

These days I am learning from mothers of all ages, in every season of motherhood. When I see new moms caring for their babies, I remember how dependent my children were in the beginning, how for those first few years Bernie and I taught them everything. New moms remind me to be dependent on God like that. My daughters are moving at lightning speed towards independence and the challenge now is to let go—to believe that what we've taught them will stick. To have confidence that even though they will make some poor choices, they will make a lot of good ones too. And I am reminded to be present in the moments, soaking in the good and the hard and the beauty and the pain, because it wasn't that long ago I was changing diapers and tying shoes.

Moms in the same stages of parenting as me let me know I'm not alone. My three daughters are in high school and college, and they are going through similar things as other kids their age. I am having similar experiences as several of my friends, and many of the issues we are facing last only for a season. C.S. Lewis nailed it when he said, "Friendship is born at that moment when one person says to another, 'What! You too? I thought I was the only one.'" I would not want to try to navigate these seasons without my friends walking alongside me.

I am learning from moms who are just a little further down the road than I am—women like my friend, Denise, who is a mom to four (now adult) boys. She tells me to pick my battles and not to sweat the small stuff. (I sweat the small stuff all the time.) When I complained that my daughter refused to wear her winter coat in the middle of a polar vortex, opting instead to wear a hoodie sweatshirt, Denise told me to let it go. "Teenagers don't wear winter coats. Let her get cold. Pick a different battle."

I'll never forget the day I told my Bible study leader I needed to drop out of her class. My girls were in preschool and I was overwhelmed. My marriage was in trouble. I was already in another moms group, and even though I really liked this teacher and enjoyed her class, I realized it was too much. When I began to unpack all of this, she looked at me with compassion and said, "How about you call me this afternoon and we can talk. I'd like to hear what's going on." *Really? I just told you I'm quitting your class and you want to take more of your time to listen to why my life feels like such a mess?* Later that afternoon, while the girls were napping, I called her, and we talked for an hour and a half. Even though her kids were grown, she had this amazing way of *remembering.* Remembering what it was like when they were little, remembering the strain parenting can put on your marriage, remembering that what most moms need more than anything else is a compassionate, listening ear. I can still remember some of the things she said to me. That was more than twenty years ago, and though she may not even remember me or our phone call, that conversation was life-changing.

My best teacher has always been my mom who, though no longer with me, mothered me with wisdom and love. It wasn't easy for her to let go as I got older. My decisions led me far from home. When she came to Dallas for my college graduation, she fully expected me to move back home to Michigan. She was totally unprepared to learn I had fallen for a guy from Mexico City and wanted to move there to study Spanish. I had no idea how hard that was for her, but she supported me. She met Bernie and welcomed him with open arms. She trusted me to make good choices and to live my life the way she'd taught me. She loved me enough to let go, to let me soar and become who God made me to be.

My mom lost her battle with cancer, but as I walked with her on her cancer journey, she continued to mother me and teach me the greatest life lessons of all. She showed me how to face challenging circumstances with faith and determination. By her example, she taught me how to live and love well, and though it broke my heart, she also taught me how to die well. She showed me a faith and trust in God that took her to the deepest places of surrender. And she demonstrated the peace that is ours when we give God everything, with open hands and a heart of abandon.

My hope is that reading this book will be a lot like that conversation with my Bible study leader. I hope you will be encouraged wherever you are on your journey. I hope these stories and truths will resonate deeply with you. I hope you will find that you are not alone in what you are going through. Motherhood is not meant to be a solo sport. Let's learn from each other. Let's be honest about the ups and downs of motherhood, marriage, and family life. Let's take a closer look at some of the "pearls of wisdom" we offer one another, be willing to laugh at some of the absurdities, and dig a little deeper to find the nuggets of truth. Being a mom is hard—maybe not the hardest job in the world, but the challenges we face as we raise our kids can stretch us to our limits. We need *real* encouragement, not fluffy platitudes that roll off the tongue but leave us feeling discouraged and alone. We need words of truth that are rooted in Scripture, words that fill us with hope and courage. Thank you for joining me on this adventure—let's get started!

#1—Enjoy Every Minute Because the Time Goes So Fast!

Enjoy *Every* Minute. Really?

> The days are long, but the years are short.
> —Gretchen Rubin

When my daughters were little, I was repeatedly given the same advice. A more "experienced" mom who was a bit further along on the motherhood journey than I was (and usually a complete stranger) would see the girls and me at the library or shopping for groceries, and she would strike up a friendly conversation. "Oh, your girls are so cute! How old are they?" She'd ask my older daughter, "Do you like being a big sister? Are you Mommy's big helper?" Then she would grow nostalgic and begin to reminisce about her own children, saying things like, "It seems like just yesterday my Susie was that little. Now she's in college. . . ." And then I knew it was coming. I knew this mom was going to look me in the eye and say with all the conviction she could muster, "Enjoy *every* minute, because the time goes so fast!" And I'd think, *I know, I know . . . it goes fast. At least that's what everyone keeps telling me. But it doesn't always feel like it's going fast with long days and sometimes longer nights of feeding, burping, and changing babies. I'm picking out*

my produce in the same clothes I slept in, and I don't remember the last time I
got more than five straight hours of sleep.

One time a woman in an elevator saw my two daughters sitting very nicely in their double stroller and said, "Oh, it's *sooo* easy when they are little like that! They listen to everything you say!" As she stepped off the elevator, I just stood there, frozen in time, thinking, *If this is so easy then I am in so much trouble!* I vowed then that I would never say such things to young moms.

Do you know who you will never hear giving this advice? Moms in the thick of it. You will not hear a mother with young children say, "Man, I don't know what is going on, but the baby was up every hour crying last night. I think he's cutting a tooth. And my three-year-old refuses to be potty trained. But you know what? I am enjoying *every* minute!" And you won't hear a mother of teenagers say, "Yep—I'm enjoying every minute! Every eye roll, every sarcastic comment, every attitude my kid throws my way . . . I'm savoring every second!"

Fast forward several years: now I am one of the more "experienced" moms. My daughters are teenagers and young adults and sometimes I want to ask, "where *has* the time gone?" Recently, while looking at a family photo from over a decade ago, I glanced over at my husband and noticed he was wearing the same shirt as in the picture! I am reminded daily of how quickly time is passing as I keep track of the mileage in my car, notice that my daughter's pants are too short (again), receive reminder calls from our dentist telling us that it's time to get our teeth cleaned, and hear the sound of my coffee maker automatically shutting off in the morning when I haven't even finished my first cup. Our mailbox is flooded with college brochures addressed to our youngest daughter, and I am still not used to her older sisters being gone.

I get it. I understand why people feel the need to point out that our children go from preschool to college in the blink of an eye. With several milestones in the rearview mirror, I agree that the years do go incredibly fast. But the moments that make up the days that make up the months that make up those years can go tiresomely slow. Motherhood is a long, sometimes lonely, road.

Blessed are those whose strength is in you,
  whose hearts are set on pilgrimage.
As they pass through the Valley of Baka (weeping),
  they make it a place of springs;
  the autumn rains also cover it with pools.
They go from strength to strength,
  till each appears before God in Zion.

(Psalm 84:5-7)

The pilgrims in this text were most likely traveling—some from very far away—to Jerusalem to worship. The word "pilgrimage" in this context refers to a long trip with a spiritual significance. That is a pretty good definition of motherhood if you ask me.

Travel in biblical times, and even a hundred years ago, was unpredictable and sometimes dangerous. Travelers did not have our current modes of transportation or the modern-day conveniences we enjoy today. They could not make reservations ahead of time. They did not have the luxuries of GPS, on-line reviews, and weather apps. Think about Mary and Joseph, arriving in Bethlehem and finding no room in any of the inns. If only they'd had a reservation and confirmation number!

These travelers are blessed (some translations use the word *happy*) because their strength is in God and their hearts are "set on pilgrimage." This little phrase captivates me. When we set our hearts on something there is a deep desire—a willingness—to go after it and make sacrifices for what we want and what matters to us. We might say, "she has her heart set on that university because they have the best nursing program in the Midwest." Or, "he has had his heart set on that cute redhead ever since he was twelve years old." When we approach parenting with our hearts set on pilgrimage, we walk with purpose. We are intentional and determined. Rather than being shortsighted, we hold the long view, "fixing our eyes on Jesus, the pioneer and perfecter of faith. For the joy set before him he endured the cross, scorning its shame, and sat down at the right hand of the throne of God" (Hebrews 12:2). Pioneer Jesus teaches us how to set our sights on something bigger than what we can see right in front of us.

When we set our hearts on pilgrimage, there is also an awareness that the journey is long, which produces patience in us. It gives us the perspective we need and helps us to "zoom the lens out." One of my favorite features of my smartphone is the ability to "zoom in" with my fingers—to make words and people's faces larger—so I can see the details with clarity. Sometimes in our daily lives, however, when we zoom in and focus on every detail of the moment (especially the hard moments), we lose sight of the bigger picture. When we live with an awareness that motherhood is a long walk, it's like zooming the lens back out. We realize everything doesn't need to get done or fixed or figured out today. We can trust God to lead us, one step at a time.

And finally, when our hearts are set on pilgrimage, there is an expectation that our journey will take us through hills and valleys and will include both smooth and rocky terrain. No one gets an easy, problem-free journey. Regardless of what we see on social media, nobody's life is picture-perfect. We all face challenges, seasons of joy and seasons of weeping, and we will not enjoy every bend of the path. Adjusting our expectations produces perseverance in us. Most of the challenges we face are temporary; we do not stay in the valleys forever.

I have kept my promise, and I do not tell young moms to enjoy every moment. I would tell a young mom to embrace each season but that it is *impossible* to enjoy every moment because some moments are terrible, and the only good thing about them is that they are momentary and do not last forever. She needs to move through them and move forward. She needs to go to sleep, wake up tomorrow and realize it's a new day, and even if she cannot see it right now, she is doing an amazing job.

I would tell her that her chatty toddler will grow up to be a chatty teenager, and she will be glad her daughter still talks to her. I would tell her that her frustrated preschooler, the one who is crying because she can't figure out how to make an airplane out of paper plates and scotch tape, will someday teach herself how to play the ukulele and knit with pencils by watching YouTube videos. And I would tell her that one day in the not-so-distant future, a teacher will say that her super-intense, over-the-top daughter—the one who told the neighbors their couch was ugly when she was in preschool—has been chosen to help a student with special needs because of her caring, kind nature.

As moms, we are given many, many moments. Some of them are more beautiful than we ever could have imagined. Some of them surprise us and catch us off guard, making us laugh until we cry, or cry until our eyes swell. And some of them are harder than we ever thought possible and bring us to our knees. They stretch us and press us and shake things out of us that we never knew were there.

It's okay to not love every minute. That's a whole lot of pressure. It is an impossible endeavor that often leaves us feeling frustrated and riddled with guilt. What if, instead, we set our hearts on pilgrimage and take each moment for what it is? What if we choose to embrace both joy and sorrow, ease and challenge, calm and chaos? What if we allow ourselves to become students again and permit our moments to be our teachers, trusting that God has drawn up the lesson plans in wisdom and love? This is how mothers become pioneers and pilgrims.

Life Boxes

My mama always said life was like a box of chocolates.
You never know what you're gonna get.
—Forrest Gump

Almost immediately after dropping off our eldest daughter, Kate, at college for her freshman year, I received an advertisement from a company that sends care packages to college students. Their products are presented in such a way that vulnerable parents, particularly mothers whose hearts have just been ripped out of their chests after sending their children hundreds of miles away from home, feel compelled to purchase one of their special packages. These care packages are designed with your child in mind (even though the "designers" have never met your child) and will be sent at precisely the right moment for when he or she is missing home, cramming for midterms, or completely stressed over final exams. You can write a personalized note to be included in the box, but the rest is all taken care of by complete strangers who do not have any idea whether your child prefers Cheetos or Fritos, Oreos or Fig Newtons, granola bars or mixed nuts. The price tag is quite hefty considering what it would cost to send your own package with your child's *actual* favorite snacks and reminders of home. I opted out and decided to put my own assortment together to send to Kate a few weeks after school started.

I began to make a list and gather some of her favorite things: Swiss Cake Rolls, Burt's Bees lip balm, English breakfast tea, York Peppermint Patties, and cozy socks. As I rummaged through kitchen cabinets and drawers looking for items to include, I came across some random junk which I decided to throw in the box as well: expired coupons, obsolete cell phone chargers, and useless objects from the junk drawer. Then, I began looking for more useless, weird things, just for fun. I went through the cabinets in the laundry room, finding all sorts of clutter and objects I knew would make Kate laugh. I cleaned the dryer filter and put the lint in a Ziploc bag. I crossed out the words "glue stick" on a fresh tube of glue and wrote "grape-flavored ChapStick" with a Sharpie. I threw in a couple stray socks and a few dead batteries for good measure, included a heart-felt note, taped the box closed and shipped it to my daughter.

She opened her special care package from us over FaceTime, and its contents made Kate and her friends laugh. Then she read the note which explained that life is a mix of both good and bad. You get some really great stuff in your life, but you also get some garbage. You will enjoy many moments in your life, but you will not enjoy them all. And a sense of humor can take you a long way.

I am a big fan of traditional wedding vows. Not everyone uses them; many couples opt to write their own vows and sometimes they do not resemble the traditional vows at all. Bernie and I wrote our own vows for our wedding, and at the time I think I was going for something softer and not as tragic sounding as "worse, poorer, sickness, and death." We pledged to support and encourage one another, to be faithful and love each other, but we did not use language that depicted the worst-case scenarios we might have to face as a couple. Now, twenty-five years later, I wish we had. Those vows would not have actually changed anything that happened, of course, but had I reflected on and absorbed the potential hardships depicted in those words and phrases, however harsh they may be, they may have prepared me a bit more for what was to come. They may have set me up to expect some incredibly hard moments mixed in with the blissful ones, instead of naively thinking we were somehow special and would escape the difficulties I had seen others face. Though it would not have lessened our grief, it might have taken away some of the shock of losing our first baby three months into my pregnancy. It might have softened the blow when a neurologist told Bernie a few years into our marriage that he had multiple sclerosis. And it might have enabled us to normalize our marital struggles instead of thinking something strange and unusual was happening to us.

What if we took vows when we became mothers? Oh, I know we wouldn't want to spoil the magic of new motherhood, with its soft blues and pinks, its nursery rhymes and lullabies. We would not want to taint our perfectly decorated nurseries with words describing the inevitable challenges of parenting. But maybe, if we had a realistic view of this motherhood journey going into it, we wouldn't beat ourselves up because we are finding some aspects of it to be harder than we ever imagined. Maybe we would not feel like we need to hide our depression or anxiety or anger over how things are not the way we thought they would be. Maybe we could lock eyes with another mom and know that we could be honest, because maybe—just maybe—she is struggling, too. If mommy vows were a thing, I think mine would read something like this:

Dear Child of mine,

I promise to love you with all my heart, no matter what. When you cuddle and coo and sleep peacefully in my arms, and when you cry all night and keep me from sleeping, I love you. When I feed you and bathe you, change you and tickle you, and when I cannot figure out for the life of me how to calm you down and make you feel better, I love you. When I am overwhelmed with both the joys and demands of caring for a totally dependent human, even in my sleep-deprived, exhausted state, I love you. When you learn to say "Mama" and say it a million times, and when you learn to say "no" and disobey me, I love you. When you figure out the keys to my heart and how to push all of my buttons, I love you. When I am funny and amaze you, when I fail and lose my temper, when I say the most beautiful words to you and then say words that should never be said, I still love you.

I will teach you wonderful things and also some not-so-wonderful things you will one day have to work very hard to unlearn. Know this: I love you. We will have such fun together and enjoy some of the very best moments this side of heaven. And there will be some really hard moments as well. We will be best buds and we will hurt one another. We will fight and struggle and need to forgive. Over and over and over again. The challenges of motherhood will bring out the very best and the very worst in me—I love you. We will grow together, learn about our great God together, and I will love you forever. No matter what.

Always,

Mama

The Valley of Weeping

As they pass through the Valley of Baka,
they make it a place of springs. . . .
—Psalm 84:6

Grown-ups are big into time travel. My friend, Denise, has four adult sons and she says if she could go back to the days when her boys were little, to the days of trick-or-treating and Santa Claus, she would do it in a heartbeat. My sister, Kari, is a baby person, and if she could travel back in time you would find her cuddling her babies in her rocking chair. She misses those days. I do not. I mean, I loved my babies, but I also love to sleep. If I could turn back time, I would go back to when my daughters were three or four years old. At this age, their personalities were really beginning to shine, and I absolutely loved their curiosity, the questions they asked, the adorable things they said, and how they seemed to hang on every word *I* said. (I know, I may not be remembering all of this exactly right, but that is part of the fun of reminiscing.) My youngest daughter, Brenna, used to say "pail nolish," and I immediately intercepted any attempt made by other people to correct her. I wanted her to say it that way forever, or at least until she could figure it out herself.

If we had magic remote controls, most of us would rewind and go back to some of these moments. We would hit "pause" from time to time, freezing the frame on certain moments that are so very special we don't want them to end. And if we are honest, there are times we would use our magic remote to fast-forward, skip over, and speed through moments and seasons that are difficult and wrought with pain.

Each of us will inevitably pass through what the Psalmist calls the "Valley of Baka" (weeping). It may be a medical or financial crisis, a period of marital distress, a betrayal, trauma, or loss. It may be a season of parenting that is especially difficult, a relational conflict, or a battle with depression or anxiety. It may be a season of loneliness or doubt—whatever it is, we wish more than anything we could just get past it as quickly as possible.

And yet the psalmist writes that "as they pass through the Valley of Baka, they make it a place of springs; the autumn rains also cover it with pools" (Psalm 84:5). Clearly, we do not relish this part of the pilgrimage. We do not enjoy our moments in the valleys. Most of us resist the process—this painful part of the journey between where we are now and where we want to be, between who we are now and who we will become. We would like to rush through it, but the valley terrain is difficult to traverse. It requires us to go slow. Yet it is in these moments, maybe more than any other, where we experience God's nearness. He never leaves us alone. He walks with us in our pain. He speaks things to us in the valley that we cannot hear anywhere else. His comfort and peace transform our valleys of weeping into places of springs.

I passed through one of my darkest valleys several years ago when I found out my mom had terminal cancer. Before I ever became a mother, I was a daughter. I was *her* daughter. And the thought of losing my mom was unbearable. There is a desperation that comes when you realize there is nothing you or any other human on the planet can do to change your situation. And though you know God can change it, and you believe he has the power to intervene and alter the outcome, the reality is that sometimes he does not. Sometimes he chooses to walk you *through* the Valley of Weeping, hold you in the darkness, and show you that he is everything you will ever need.

I wanted to fast-forward through the pain and the sorrow. I did not want to watch my mom suffer. I did not want to watch her die. I told my closest friends, "If I could skip over all of it I would. I'd go straight to the funeral. And then I would probably want to skip the funeral too, because the whole wretched ordeal seems intolerable."

And yet, as I leaned into the hard moments and made my way through the rocky, uneven places, one foot in front of the other, my valley became a place of springs. Time with my mom was a gift. Friends came alongside, supported me, cared for me, and walked with me. God's presence brought healing and comfort. He filled me with unexpected joy and an abundance of peace. His love enveloped and held me together, and in him, I found everything I needed.

It's a good thing we do not have a magic remote control. Because often it can be so hard for us to see the value, the beauty, and the opportunities for growth in the less-than-perfect moments. If it were up to us, we might choose only those moments that are shiny and pretty at first glance, ordering up exactly what seems good to us, and then replaying them over and over again. We might be tempted to skip over those moments that loom dark in the distance and threaten to bring pain, struggle, anxiety, or sadness into our lives. But God is in all of it: the good and the bad, the joy and the sorrow, the beauty and the pain. He is good. He brings joy. He creates beauty.

If we want to live authentic lives in the real world, with our real families and our real problems, enjoying every minute is not an attainable goal. Let's instead resolve to be present, not longing for the past or anxiously thinking about the days to come. Let's enjoy and savor and soak up every second of the beautiful moments because they are a gift, and let's persevere and grow through the hard ones. Let's put our trust in the Giver of moments who walks with us, loves us with an everlasting love, and is able to transform our valleys into places of springs.

> See, I am doing a new thing!
> > Now it springs up; do you not perceive it?
> I am making a way in the wilderness
> > and streams in the wasteland.

(Isaiah 43:19)

Review:

When our hearts are "set on pilgrimage," it changes the way we view parenting. Rather than being short-sighted, we hold the long view. We develop patience and endurance as we "zoom the lens out," remembering that motherhood is a long walk. We find our strength in God as we walk one step at a time. And we adjust our expectations to include both hills and valleys, smooth and rocky terrain, seasons of joy, and seasons of weeping. We will not enjoy every moment of this journey, but we can find joy along the way.

Reflect:

1. How does "setting your heart on pilgrimage" shift the way you view your parenting journey? In which of these areas do you need God to expand your perspective: holding the long view (zooming the lens out), walking each step in his strength, or adjusting your expectations?

2. In the Introduction, Becky talked about how some of the platitudes we offer one another can produce guilt-laced, negative self-talk. What does your internal self-talk sound like? (Examples may include: *I should be enjoying my kids more. This shouldn't be so hard. I should be a better mom.* . . .)

3. When have you wished you could fast-forward through a valley? Have you experienced God's presence in places of pain?

Respond:

Father, you are full of compassion,
I commit and commend myself unto you,
in whom I am, and live, and know.
Be the goal of my pilgrimage, and my Rest by the way.
Let my soul take refuge from the crowding turmoil
of worldly thoughts beneath the shadow of your wings;
let my heart, this sea of restless waves,
find peace in you, O God. Amen.

—St. Augustine

#2—God Will Never Give You More Than You Can Handle

Weak Made Strong

Do you not know? Have you not heard?
The LORD is the everlasting God,
the Creator of the ends of the earth.
He will not grow tired or weary,
and his understanding no one can fathom.
He gives strength to the weary
and increases the power of the weak.
—Isaiah 40:28-29

My sister, Kari, has five children with an age span between them of seven years. She has heard just about every variation of the idea that God won't give us more than we can handle. "God must have known you could handle all those kids or he wouldn't have given them to you!" Or, "You know what the Good Book says! The Good Lord won't give you more than you can handle!" Or this one, which makes her feel like a total hypocrite: "I know you must be the best mom ever and your kids must love you so much since God blessed you with so many!!" At which point she wants to make a public service announcement to everyone within earshot that it's actually quite the opposite in real life. She wants to say, "Actually I think I'm a *worse* mom because I have so many kids that stretch me so thin I want to pull my hair out. My husband and I actually asked the kids the other night, 'If you could live with one of your friends, would you want to?' Four out of the five said yes and Maggie (the youngest) was on the fence . . . depending on how often she could visit us."

One evening many years ago, Bernie and I gathered with a group of couples from our church, and one of the couples announced they were expecting their second child. We were all in various stages of beginning our families at that point, and while I was excited to hear their news, I was feeling particularly sensitive towards a couple in our group who had been trying for quite some time to get pregnant. They had been open about their struggles with infertility and the lengths they were taking to have a baby. Which is why I winced when the group member who was expecting his second child said, "The Lord has seen fit to bless us with another child—he must know we can handle it." Sometimes we say things without thinking about who is listening or how our words may land. I remember thinking that comment might have stung for the childless couple, the implication being that the Lord didn't see fit to bless them with their first child, because maybe they wouldn't be able to handle it.

During my first pregnancy, I stayed up late most nights reading the mother of all pregnancy manuals: *What to Expect When You're Expecting*. The information in that book confirmed that some of the things I was worrying about could, in fact, happen, and my eyes were also opened to a myriad of other problems and complications I had no idea were even possibilities. I stopped using artificial sweeteners and slept only on my left side to increase blood flow to the baby. I took my prenatal vitamins religiously and made sure to get plenty of rest. I avoided raising my arms above my head because my grandmother insisted it could cause a miscarriage, and I tried the best I could to prepare myself for becoming a mother.

Except I didn't get to become a mother, at least not that time. Bernie and I arrived at our 12-week check-up with a VHS tape in tow, ready to record our baby's ultrasound. But instead of getting to see our baby doing in utero gymnastics, the ultrasound confirmed there was no heartbeat. The baby had died a couple of weeks earlier, and once my body figured out what was happening, I was going to have a miscarriage. We left the doctor's office with our empty VHS tape and our empty dreams, and I wondered in the days that followed what I had done to cause my baby to stop growing past nine and a half weeks. Maybe I raised my arms over my head to put away the dishes because I forgot how disastrous a move like that could be. It felt like a mean trick or a terrible joke, and in the deepest parts of me, I wondered what I had done to deserve such a loss. I considered the possibility that maybe God didn't think I was ready to be a mom, but then he surely also would have known I wasn't ready to lose a baby, either.

That wasn't the first time I had faced a problem or trial too heavy for me to bear. It wasn't the first time I had tried to interpret God's will or motives or heart for me in light of my circumstances. I grieved for months, and most people didn't get it. They didn't understand how it could hurt so much when I never even held my baby. They'd say things like, "You're young. You can have another one," as if the loss of this baby's life didn't matter and a future pregnancy was guaranteed. Whenever someone quipped with the scientific reason, "It's just nature's way of taking care of some kind of abnormality," that didn't set well with me, either. *If this is just a natural occurrence, why is everything in me crying out for my baby?* After a while, folks seemed to be bothered or surprised that I was still feeling my little one's absence. "Oh, you're still not over it?" Feelings don't work like switches, and grief doesn't follow a straight, predictable line.

The only comfort I found was in drawing near to God, although it was difficult for me to go to church each week and see my friend, one of the worship leaders, who found out she was pregnant right around the same time as me. Our due dates were within days of one another, and every week, as I saw her belly get bigger, the ache inside of me felt like it was getting bigger too. The questions and resentment and perceived lack of fairness—it was all more than I could handle. So I didn't handle it. I continually turned toward God and asked him for help. I gave my burdens to him. I prayed for strength and peace. I asked him to heal me.

Whether it's in the daily grit of being a mom—when we feel like we are sinking and have no idea what we are doing and can't get the baby to stop crying and how is it possible that these kids can eat so much and we just wish we could go to the bathroom alone and have a few moments to ourselves—or in the bigger losses, disappointments, struggles, and burdens, if we are trying to "handle" things on our own, we are in for trouble.

God never meant for us to handle things on our own. He doesn't give us burdens in proportion to our capacity to bear them. He doesn't play games or do cruel tricks. He's not a terrible prankster. He allows us to walk through some really hard moments, even seasons, but he walks with us through it all. We may cry out, "This is too hard! This burden is too heavy to bear. I'm too exhausted to carry it." He knows. He wants us to lay it down. He responds, "My grace is sufficient for you, for my power is made perfect in weakness" (2 Cor. 12:9).

When we are in over our heads, feel overwhelmed, and our burdens are more than we can bear, we are in the best possible place for God to showcase his strength in and through our lives.

Running

Even youths grow tired and weary,
and young men stumble and fall;
but those who hope in the LORD
will renew their strength.
They will soar on wings like eagles;
they will run and not grow weary,
they will walk and not be faint.
—Isaiah 40:30-31

I do not like to run. Ever since I was a kid, running long distances has been something I try to avoid. Now, as a middle-aged woman, I can imagine only a couple of scenarios that would cause me to run: if I were being chased by a Rottweiler or in danger of missing my flight. Several years ago, however, when my kids were in grade school, I dabbled. I kind of got into it. Up until that point, my exercise routine had been brisk walking. Whether on my treadmill or around my neighborhood, I loved the physical activity and the time to think, pray, and enjoy some solitude.

One day, I tried a program on my treadmill that alternated between walking and running, as well as changing the incline to create a more productive work-out. After each short period of running, I literally breathed a "thank you" to the machine for allowing me to walk again. When I was done with my work-out, however, I realized there were aspects of running that I actually enjoyed: pushing myself to the limit, working my body in new ways, and the invigoration I felt when I broke a sweat, my heart rate was up, and my breathing was sharpened. Over the next several weeks I experimented. I tried out different programs on my treadmill and started regularly walking/running in my neighborhood, surprised by an activity I never thought I could enjoy.

During this brief period of athleticism, I discovered a trick that helped me persevere a little while longer when I didn't think I could make it to the end of my route. When everything in me wanted to quit, I'd set my eyes on a location just up ahead. Instead of stopping, I would choose a park or an intersection—or even the end of the next block—and tell myself I could make it a little bit further. And I could. I could not have run a marathon or even a 5K during that season, but I found I could always go just a little further when I felt like quitting. I don't know if real runners use this technique, but it worked really well for me. What is true in running is also true in life. This is what persevering in parenting and marriage looks like.

During our hardest season of marriage, I remember thinking, *I can't do this anymore. This is where most people would walk away and call it quits. This is where most people would cite "irreconcilable differences." It feels unbearably hard.* On those days, the thought of staying married fifty more years seemed like an impossible feat. But in one of my most desperate moments, I realized a hope-infusing truth: *I don't need to stay married for fifty more years right now. I need to stay married for one more month. One more week. One more day. God can help me do that.*

On my worst days as a mom, when I have run out of patience and I am doubting my competency and it feels like I am getting it all wrong, the future can seem overwhelming. *What kind of mom will I be when my kids are teenagers if I can't even handle them as preschoolers? How on earth are we going to put these kids through college? How will they ever become productive members of society when I can't even get them to clean their rooms?*

Again, when I choose a closer goal, I find the strength to go a little bit further. I may not have the capabilities right now to raise these kids and launch them into the world, but God will give me the strength I need *today* to bathe them, feed them, and put them to bed. He will give me the wisdom I need for this hard conversation. He will give me the strength I need tomorrow and the day after that and the day after that—new mercies each morning and grace in each moment to do what is next—to do what is right in front of me. I can stop panicking. I can silence the *what ifs?* I can breathe.

By shortening the goal and focusing on a closer target, I find hope. I can always go a little further. I may not know how I will make it the distance, but I will choose today to say a kind word, to forgive again, to serve someone I don't feel like serving. I will choose to do something to take care of myself. I will pray for strength and guidance once more. I'll call a friend, take a walk, go to church, attend a support group or counseling appointment one more time. I will open my heart once again, and in this moment, I will surrender to the One who can lead me to a better place. Taking small steps and doing the next right thing gives me hope.

Sometimes we may feel like we are running alone, but we are never alone. In our weakest moments God is at work, ever-present with us, giving us the strength we need to persevere. As we look up and fix our eyes on Jesus, the author and perfecter of our faith, he helps us endure when we most feel like quitting. And throughout Scripture we see his desire that we run this race together, supporting one another and cheering each other on.

Many years ago, our family experienced the excitement of cheering on a couple of our relatives as they ran in the Chicago Marathon. Even though our daughters were very young at the time, they remember heading into the city to find our runners. We calculated the approximate time our relatives would reach certain mile markers, and then drove and parked our car near those locations. We then made our way through the crowds and scanned the runners' faces looking for our people. I was surprised by how emotional I felt as I watched hundreds of runners, some of them so obviously weary and exhausted, stride—even stumble—past us. Some of them had their names printed on their jerseys, and I'd find myself shouting encouragements to complete strangers. "Way to go Michael! You're doing great! Keep going!!" And, "You can do it Maria—don't give up! You've got this!!" A couple times my words caught in my throat as I choked back tears. We held up signs we had made with the names of our loved ones, and when we finally spotted them, you would have thought we hadn't seen them in decades or they had just come back from war as we jumped up and down, whooping and hollering. They later told us the encouragement and cheers from the crowd helped them tremendously to keep going and to finish the race.

Maybe it was because I was in the throes of mothering young children. Maybe it was because I was sleep deprived, exhausted, and depleted, stumbling along in my own race. Whatever the reasons, that experience marked me. More than just a fun family moment, it was a beautiful picture to me of what it means to be running this race *together*. This is what we do for each other as brothers and sisters in Christ. As we encourage and cheer each other on, we find strength to persevere and keep going. We are revitalized and energized to go a little further. And as we model this for our children, something extraordinary happens. Moment by moment, grace by grace, as we run our race with the strength God provides, we pass on a baton of humility to our children. As they see us depend on God in our weaknesses and mutually encourage and support one another, they learn that struggle and perseverance are part of the journey. They experience first-hand the importance and value of community. They realize they don't have to run their race alone, in their own strength. They can humbly ask for help when they need it and learn to rely on God, who provides everything we need to run the race set before us.

Bad Things Happen
to Good Families

God is our refuge and strength,
an ever-present help in trouble.
—Psalm 46:1

Carrying a plate of freshly baked cookies, I feel my
emotions begin to fray as I walk up the driveway and lightly
tap on their front door. We don't know each other well, but
we've known each other for nearly twenty years. Our families
both have three children; our older girls just beginning their
adult lives, theirs in their late twenties and early thirties. A
few days earlier, their family was ripped apart when their
thirty-year-old son died by suicide.

Of course everyone wants to do something, but nobody
knows quite what to do or what to say. One of the women
in our circle is eighty-five years old. She had brought them a
giant pan of lasagna the day before and said if each of us
could take turns bringing something every day for the next
week, they'd be covered. She was doing what her generation
knew how to do so well: show up with food and love people.
She had suggested I make cookies for them.

Sometimes, in situations like this, I don't know what to do
so I talk myself out of doing anything. I nearly talked myself
out of making the cookies, because I was afraid of doing the
wrong thing. *I really don't know them very well. I don't want to be intrusive
or invade their privacy. I don't even know what kind of food they like to eat, or
if they have allergies. And besides, they probably don't have any appetite right*

now anyway . . . Sometimes it's easier to do nothing, to keep a bit of distance.

I couldn't stop thinking about their family. I prayed for them, although my prayers felt weak. Then, on my day off from work, since I had all the ingredients in my pantry and my elderly friend reminds me of my grandmother, I took her suggestion and baked the cookies.

Now, as I approach their front door, the reality of the hell they must be living through begins to hit me. I can't even imagine. I don't want to *let* myself imagine. The door opens and I am invited in. And as I step inside their entryway, I am pulled in—just for a few minutes—to the devastation this couple is facing. The confusion. The disbelief. The seemingly unbearable pain of not only losing their beloved son, but losing him *this way*. I listen. I cry with them. I am almost embarrassed by my cookies—why on earth would I think they would even want to eat them? It is a gesture more than it is sustenance of any kind, and one that opens up an invitation for me to simply stand with them and say, "I'm so, so sorry." When I leave, I tell them I will pray for them. In the days, weeks, and months that follow, I do pray for them, because this is a consuming grief with the power to swallow them whole. This is too much to bear.

Bad things—terrible, tragic, horrendous things—happen to good people and to good families. In moments like these, we may want to console people with a nice, neat cliché. But the idea that God doesn't give us more than we can handle is at best an empty platitude, and at worst a hurtful lie. We were not made to "handle" sickness, evil, and death. We were not designed to carry burdens that break us. We want to tell people that God won't give them more than they can handle because we want them to know they will get through it. We want them to believe they will survive. But the hard, saving-grace truth is that the only way any of us survive the unbearable pain this life throws our way is by crying out to God for help, and by allowing others to come alongside us in our darkest moments. We say, "This is too heavy! I cannot possibly bear the weight of this on my own. I need help. I cannot do this alone."

Contrary to what many people think, "God will never give you more than you can handle" is not in the Bible. Rather, Scripture is full of stories of individuals who were, in fact, given more than they could handle: Moses, David, Mary, Paul. They all said, essentially, "I cannot do this in my own strength. I need your strength to carry this." The apostle Paul, when given a "thorn in his flesh" (people debate what this thorn might be, but does it really matter?), asks God to take it from him. He cries out to God as many of us have done in our despair—*This is too hard. This is too heavy. I don't want it. I hate it! Take it from me. Deliver me from it. Heal me. Remove it from my life.* Three times God responds to Pauls' plea, "My grace is enough for you. My power is made perfect in your weakness." And he says the same to us.

We tend to place our focus on our ability—or lack of ability—to bear the weight of our burdens. Our despair overwhelms us because deep down we know we cannot carry such weight for any distance at all. Our only hope is to look up, to fix our gaze on the One who never grows weary and whose strength never runs out.

Always Use the Buddy System

Two people are better off than one . . . . If one person
falls, the other can reach out and help.
—Ecclesiastes 4:9-10, NLT

When I was a kid we were taught to "always use the buddy system." Whether we were swimming, riding bikes, or running around the neighborhood, we knew there was safety and strength in numbers. Teachers implemented the buddy system on school field trips to help keep track of their students, and at school we often worked in pairs or groups to complete projects and tasks.

This idea originated with God. The Bible is filled with examples of God calling someone to do something, and then provided a "buddy" to walk alongside. In the beginning, God said it was not good for man to be alone, so he created Eve to walk alongside Adam. When God called Moses to lead over a million people out of slavery, Moses argued that he was unqualified to do the assignment God was giving him. So his brother Aaron came alongside to help and to speak on his brother's behalf. And in the beautiful story of Naomi and Ruth, Naomi tried to persuade her daughter-in-law to go back to her original family after both their husbands had died. But Ruth refused, telling her mother-in-law, "Don't urge me to leave you or to turn back from you. Where you go I will go, and where you stay I will stay. Your people will be my people and your God my God. Where you die I will die, and there I will be buried (Ruth 1:16-17)." They journeyed together, and God made a way for these two women of faith.

Queen Esther was a brave and wise young woman, but she did not save her people on her own. Her cousin, Mordecai, was the one who uncovered the plot to kill the Jews and shared this vital information with Esther, who was in a position to do something about it. It was Mordecai who encouraged her with these faith-filled, history-altering words, "And who knows but that you have come to your royal position for such a time as this?" (Esther 4:14). The word "encourage" means "to fill with or inspire courage." As Mordecai *encouraged* Esther to be brave and see where and how God was at work, we also need people to inspire courage and speak words of truth in our lives.

When Mary, the mother of Jesus, was told she would become pregnant by the Holy Spirit and give birth to the Son of God, no one believed her, at least not at first. So Mary went to visit her relative Elizabeth, who was advanced in years and faith. Elizabeth believed Mary—she was experiencing a miracle herself, becoming pregnant in her old age! What a gift God gave these women in one another, allowing them to walk together as they fully surrendered to the God for whom nothing is impossible.

One of my favorite Bible stories as a child was "The Boy Jesus at the Temple." In this story, Jesus' parents and family set out on a pilgrimage to Jerusalem to worship. On their way back home, a day into their journey, they realized they had lost track of Jesus. Mary and Joseph lost track of the 12-year-old *Son of God!* As a child, I loved this story because it made Jesus' family seem a little more normal, not so different from my own. After three days of searching, they finally found Jesus, teaching in the temple. In addition to some fascinating family dynamics that played out, one thing that strikes me about this story is that Mary and Joseph lost track of Jesus "because they assumed he was among the other travelers" (Luke 2:44, New Living Translation). This speaks to the type of community they were a part of. They were not traveling alone; they belonged to a group of people who looked out for one another.

Even Jesus, as he began his earthly ministry, did not do it alone. He could have, but instead, he hand-picked a group of ordinary men and women in need of a savior to be his disciples and friends. On the night he was betrayed, arrested, and then crucified, his disciples went with him to a garden to pray. He asked his friends to stay with him and keep watch with him. He told them to pray for themselves, so they would not fall into temptation. Scripture tells us he was overwhelmed with sorrow to the point of death, and he did not have the strength to do what was coming. The weight of the burden was too much for him to bear. In the most vulnerable of prayers he pours out his humanness, his weakness, and his despair. "Father, if you are willing, take this cup from me; yet not my will, but yours be done.' An angel from heaven appeared to him and strengthened him" (Luke 22:42-43). Notice the progression here: he vulnerably admits and confesses his weakness; he chooses to obey and do the will of his Father; he is given the strength he needs to do that which, moments earlier, felt unbearable.

Many years ago, after attending a marriage workshop at our church, Bernie and I became apprentice leaders, and then leaders. It has been our privilege to walk alongside couples who are seeking growth and healing in their marriages. Early on, I had this faulty idea that marriage ministry leaders would have it all together. They would be people who had fixed all their problems and could now help other people fix theirs. I could not have been more wrong. Over the years, we have continued to need the help this ministry provides. At times, we have found ourselves back in the participants' seats, needing guidance and support. More than once, we have been encouraged to take a break from leading in order to nurture our own marriage, which has created a culture within our ministry of authenticity and honesty. These fellow leaders have become family to us. We don't have to pretend things are great just because we are leaders. We don't need to hide when we are struggling just because people are counting on us to serve.

A couple of years ago, on a Friday morning, Bernie and I got into a fight. We stopped it from escalating and both left for work, but we were angry all day. We had a marriage event scheduled for that evening, and this wasn't the first time we had had a conflict before going to serve at an event. There is even a running joke among the leaders in our circle that marital conflict is a given on days when we have a workshop or event. Even still, we felt the urgency and the frustration of having to fix things in a hurry. We had actually been bickering and arguing for most of that week, so there was an accumulation of misunderstandings, frustrations, and hurt on both sides. The argument that morning wasn't only about that one thing. It was about the thing that happened the day before, and the other thing that had happened a couple of days before that. Frequent smaller arguments have a way of snowballing into larger conflicts, and by the time I got home from work, we had a boulder-sized offense between us. We were both still very upset, and we were supposed to lead a table that night. We tried to talk in the car but ended up arguing the entire duration of the twenty-minute drive to church. By the time we pulled into the church parking lot, we were in a full-blown fight, far worse than the one we had started that morning. We were both defensive, raising our voices and speaking to one another with contempt. We were doing all of the things we knew we should not be doing.

As Bernie pulled our car into the parking spot and turned off the engine, I stated what I thought was obvious. "We can't go in there. We can't lead a table when we are at each other's throats." And yet, I also knew that we *needed* to go in there. Our speaker was teaching about conflict and communication, and we needed to hear what he had to say. We needed to learn how to improve in both these areas. So I said to Bernie,

"But we need to be here. We need to hear the teaching and find a way to get to a better place."

We got out of the car and walked across the parking lot, continuing to sputter comments under our breath, and as I opened the door to the church, Bernie muttered something about how he should just leave and I should take an Uber home. I stopped mid-stride and glared at my husband as I let the door go. As we turned around and walked back to our car, I thought, *We can't even get through the doors. How did this become such a mess?*

We sat in the car for a few more minutes, now late for the leaders' meeting, and I decided I would go to the event by myself and catch a ride home with someone. So I got out of the car and retraced my steps, stopping halfway between the car and the church entrance. *I don't want to walk in there alone and have to ask someone for a ride home. I don't want to have to explain to our friends why Bernie isn't here. I guess it would be easier to just go home.*

At that moment, our friend, Steve, came walking out of the church and met me in the middle of the parking lot. Steve is a strong, silent type, and we have known him and his wife Karen for a long time. He was serving that evening as a greeter, as he often did, welcoming people as they walked through the doors. He had probably seen us pull in, get out of our car, walk up to the church while saying a few choice words with body language to match, then turn around and go back to our car. When he saw me get out of the car a second time and start walking again, he probably thought, *Good grief. What is going on here?*

"Do you want me to go talk to him?" he asked.

"I don't know, Steve, he's pretty mad. We are just in a really bad place, and I don't know if he wants to talk." Steve said he would go see, and I went to sit on a bench to pray. Except I didn't pray. I sat there instead, allowing shame and defeat to have a conversation in my head. *Here you are again. How pathetic. You'd think after almost twenty years you'd be able to make it to a marriage event and walk through those doors. You really should just go home. You don't belong here. You guys will never get it.*

A few minutes later, I saw Bernie get out of the car and walk into the church. He didn't see me, and I didn't know where Steve was. I just knew that now one of us was inside, so I stood up and made my way through the door. Bernie was by the entrance with Steve, who greeted me with a hug. I told Steve and some of the other leaders that we were there as participants. We couldn't lead a table, but we needed to be there. (Steve later told me how thrilled he was when Bernie and I both decided to walk through those doors and just "be" rather than "do".) These leaders came around us without judgement and told us that they have been in our shoes. They normalized our struggle and identified with our pain. They loved us right where we were, for exactly who we were in that moment. This is the body of Christ. This is what it looks like for God to give us strength and help when our burdens are too great to bear on our own.

We listened to the teaching, and then, during the small group time, Bernie and I moved to the back of the room. We asked each other for forgiveness. We began the first of many conversations to get back to a better place. We left that event grateful that we had come, our hearts measurably softer than when we had arrived. We needed to be there. I will never forget that night. I will never forget Steve walking out to the parking lot to get us because we couldn't get through the doors on our own.

After Jesus surrendered to the will of his Father, he was strengthened by an angel. He was then arrested and led away like a criminal. Many of his disciples fled and scattered that night. At the very end, only a few faithful followers were gathered at the foot of the cross, including John, the beloved disciple of Jesus, and Mary, the Lord's mother who, as a young virgin, had said, "I am the Lord's servant." Before Jesus was born—before he was even conceived—Mary had already surrendered her will to her heavenly Father's. She had chosen a blessed, but oh-so difficult, path. As she watched her beloved son be crucified before her eyes, what was being required of her was more than she could bear on her own. In the final moments before Jesus died, in a stunning dialogue that demonstrated the depths of his love for those gathered at the cross, he saw his mother there, and John standing nearby, and he said to her, "Dear woman, here is your son." And to John he said, "Here is your mother" (John 19:26-27, NLT). Moments before they watched him breathe his last, he was telling them to take care of each other, to be a family and help each other through.

Scripture is clear: God never intended for us to walk alone. He knows we need each other. He calls us to walk alongside and bear one another's burdens. He empowers us to inspire courage in one another and speak truth. He leads us to step into the hard moments and painful places, to bring lasagna and cookies, to show up even when it's hard and no one knows what to do or say, and to walk out to the parking lot to get our friends who can't make it into the building on their own. He calls us to become family to those who are hurting.

Review:

God never said he wouldn't give us more than we can handle, and he never meant for us to handle things on our own. He doesn't give us burdens in proportion to our capacity to bear them, but rather, he walks *with us* through our hardest moments and seasons, making the unbearable somehow bearable. Whether it's in the daily grit of being a mom or in the bigger losses, disappointments, struggles, and burdens, if we are trying to "handle" things on our own, we are in for trouble. He gives us strength when we are weak (2 Corinthians 12:9), and he calls us to bear one another's burdens when they are too heavy to carry alone (Galatians 6:2).

Reflect:

1. In what areas of life do you tend to try to handle things alone? When are you most resistant to ask for help—from God and from others?

2. In moments when you feel overwhelmed, how can you "shorten the goal" and "focus on a closer target," as Becky referenced in the chapter *Running*?

3. Who is walking with you on your motherhood journey? What practical steps can you take to strengthen and cultivate relationships with others?

Respond:

God, thank you that I am never alone because you are with me. When life's burdens are more than I can bear, help me to find my strength in you. Search me and know my heart. Show me when I am trying to handle things in my own strength, and reveal my tendencies towards self-sufficiency. May my children see me live in daily dependence on you and walk in humility with others on this journey. Amen.

#3—A Mother's Love Is Totally Pure and Selfless

Moms are Human, Too

All these people keep waxing sentimental about how fabulously well I am doing as a mother, how competent I am, but I feel inside like when you're first learning to put nail polish on your right hand with your left. You can do it, but it doesn't look all that great around the cuticles.

—Anne Lamott

Years ago, an older woman in my Bible study said something that shocked me. After a lively conversation about parenting, and with a dreamy tone in her voice, she said, "You know, a mother's love is the *only* love that is totally pure and selfless." Several women around the table nodded their heads in agreement, but if I had taken a sip of my coffee at that exact moment I probably would have sprayed it all over the table. I remember thinking, *Either they are delusional, or I am unusually wicked!*

I agree that a mother's love is like no other. A mother's love is tender and nurturing, unconditional, and stronger than the grave. While I am continually making sacrifices for my children, I don't think I can honestly claim *total* selflessness considering I rode into Mommy-ville on a pony named Epidural. Calling for the anesthesiologist while in labor with each of my three daughters was entirely about me and my overwhelming desire to be relieved of the otherworldly pain of childbirth. As my babies have grown over the years, I couldn't even begin to count the number of times I've reacted out of fear or anger in a parenting situation, or made a decision based on what worked for me at that moment. I can never claim that everything I do is for my kids, because that is simply not true.

I have never once taken my kids to Six Flags Great America, because I think one of the great things about living in America is that we don't have to go to Six Flags if we don't want to. I hate carnivals and amusement parks. For years, my children didn't even know we had a carnival in our town called "Frontier Days" because I took an alternate route home during the week of July 4th so they wouldn't see the rides and the people and the cotton candy. I've chosen to watch HGTV instead of playing pretend. I've RSVP'd "no" to kids' birthday parties because I didn't want to go hang out with the other moms and put myself in an awkward social situation. And more than once I've ordered Cadbury chocolate eggs online—the ones with the crispy shell and rich chocolatey center—and stashed them in an inconspicuous place where my daughters wouldn't find them, even though I know they love them just as much as I do.

There's more, *so much more*, but you get the idea. Even when it may look like I am doing everything for my kids, my motives may be askew. I am sometimes so uncomfortable with the feeling of my child being upset that I'll do whatever it takes to make her or keep her happy with me. In those moments, avoiding a conflict or unpleasant situation takes precedence over good parenting. Other times, I find it too painful to see my kids suffer consequences or face hard realities, so I step in and try to rescue. Without even realizing I'm doing it, I get in God's way and short-circuit the thing he is trying to accomplish in my child's life because I am afraid or impatient.

I am pretty sure I am not alone in this. Yes, moms are irreplaceable. Moms have an unparalleled level of influence in their children's lives. However, with that influence comes the potential for a whole lot of ugly: mom guilt, manipulation, selfish motives, and the desire for control. Moms are not saints; moms are human. Humans are sinful. Only God's love is truly perfect, and we need his help to love well. We need his perfect love to drive us—to be the motivating force for good as we love our children.

Slamming Doors and Repairing Relationships

Everyone should be quick to listen,
slow to speak, and slow to anger,
for man's anger does not bring about
the righteousness that God desires.
—James 1:19-20, BSB

I like to slam doors when I get really mad. I'm not proud of it, and it's not a behavior I want my kids to adopt, but I cannot deny the feeling of satisfaction I get when I hear that door slam and I know I've put it out there—to the person with whom I'm angry or to the universe if I'm alone—"Let the record show that I am upset. I am very, *very* upset!"

I'll never forget the first time I lost my temper in front of my daughter, Kate. She was only six months old and I was in hysterics because she had been diagnosed with her first ear infection. (Yes, I was *that* kind of first-time mother.) My pediatrician prescribed an antibiotic, but my chiropractor told me not to give it to her. He said he could correct the problem through a chiropractic manipulation and that the antibiotic would mess up her digestive system and cause more problems. I felt confused and, for some reason, guilty that I had allowed her to get sick. Even as I write these words, I know this is ridiculous, but moms have a way of blaming themselves for all sorts of things that are in no way their fault. I decided to go with the pediatrician's recommendation and measured out the correct dose of the liquid medication. Kate was in a baby seat and as soon as I began to tip the spoon dispenser to pour the medicine into her mouth, her tongue pushed back in protest. She jerked her head slightly to the right and the sticky, syrupy liquid ran down her chin, soaking into her shirt. I panicked. I pulled the dispenser back and half the liquid was gone. Not only would my daughter not cooperate, but I didn't know how much she had ingested. Should I hold her down and pour a full dose down her throat? Should I just give her half a dose? I didn't know what to do.

As a first-time mom, I had unreasonable expectations on myself, and for reasons that don't make sense to me now, I felt like a failure in that moment. I felt scared because my daughter had an infection and had been up all night crying, and I couldn't get her to take the medicine she needed. I was faced with the reality that I was not in control of this little person who meant more to me than anyone in the world. In frustration, I stormed into the kitchen and grabbed the dirty frying pan off the stove. The remnants of our scrambled eggs from breakfast that morning somehow made me even more angry, and I threw the pan into the sink and started yelling. I slammed the kitchen cabinet door and yelled some more. My eyes filled with tears, and my yelling turned to sobbing as I caught Kate's face out of the corner of my eye. She was still in her baby seat and she was watching me, wide-eyed with alarm. At once, I stopped myself and thought, *she's young. She won't remember this. I'll never lose it like this in front of her again.*

But I did lose it again. And again and again. When she refused to listen as a preschooler, when I caught her lying to me in middle school, and when her disrespectful attitude in her teen years set me off, I lost it. When Kate was fifteen, we began fighting more frequently, and one day as I stormed out of her room, I slammed her door. I had done it before, but this time, when the wooden frame hanging on her wall came crashing to the floor, I knew I had gone too far. The frame was special to her; it held a collage of photos of her and her sister, Claire, and it had been hanging in her room since she started sleeping in a big girl bed.

I opened the door and apologized. The frame was intact, and I told her I wouldn't do it again. But a couple months later we had a fight that was even bigger and uglier and blew all our other fights out of the water. Beneath my anger was my fear, which threatened to swallow me up. I was afraid Kate was losing her way. I was afraid I was a horrible mother. I was afraid we would never get back to a better place in our relationship. As I stormed out of her room that day, I was filled with regret the moment I felt her door leave my hands. I waited for the slam and then I cringed, anticipating the sound of the frame hitting the floor. After the crash I heard Kate cry out, "You did it again!" and this time, I broke the frame. Even worse, I broke her heart.

I had known for years that I had a problem with anger. Though anger is a normal, human emotion, God tells us not to sin in our anger. He tells us to get rid of destructive anger and rage, to throw off the sin that so easily entangles us, and to be controlled by his spirit. God's anger is righteous. His anger is controlled. His anger is justified. My anger, however, is usually rooted in selfishness. I don't like the way someone is acting or their attitude toward me. I don't get my way. Sometimes, like the day I broke the frame, my anger is fueled by my fear and the terrible realization that I am not in control.

We didn't talk about what happened for the first couple of days after the incident, beyond me apologizing profusely for doing precisely what I said I wouldn't do. I told her it wouldn't happen again, but she didn't believe me. Why should she? I would have to do more than tell her; I would have to show her. I promised myself I wouldn't ever slam her door again. My heart was truly repentant. Though I had always known that losing my temper like that was not good, I saw with clarity that my anger does not bring about the righteous life that God desires. It will never bring about the relationship I want with my daughter. It will never create the trusting, loving, safe relationship we both desire. Sinning in my anger costs me something precious. Broken relationships are too high a price to pay for the momentary relief of unleashing my anger.

A few days after our fight, Kate approached me with caution. "Do you think you could help me fix my frame?" She was offering me an olive branch, and I took it. It was grace.

We sat, mostly in silence, at the dining room table as we worked together to repair the wooden frame. We filled in the cracks with wood filler, and then I used a Q-tip to apply stain over the scratches while Kate followed with a rag. As we repaired the frame, I thought about how God repairs us and our relationships. As a mom, I have missed the mark more times than I can count. I've fallen short over and over again. God, in his grace, fills in the gaps. Through Christ, my sins are cleansed and forgiven. He restores what is broken and is making all things new.

That frame still hangs on Kate's bedroom wall. It still has some visible scratches, and it is now part of our story. When she left for college, the pain I felt wasn't only because my firstborn was flying the coop. It hurt because I wished things between us were better. Her first Christmas back home was rough, but we continued to come back to the table to do the repair work in our relationship. We kept talking and forgiving and seeking to understand one another.

On a mid-summer day between Kate's freshman and sophomore year, I remember pulling the car over after picking her up from work. We were fighting again, and looking at my daughter was like looking into a mirror; her anger reflected mine. The hurt in her voice echoed my own. This relationship was not what we wanted, but what we wanted was worth fighting for.

After moving her into her dorm room for her second year, I placed a card on her desk before we said our goodbyes. As I hugged my daughter one last time, she slipped a card into my hand and said, "Read this in the car." As my husband pulled out of the parking lot, I read the words I had longed to hear a year earlier, but they meant even more that second year because of all we had worked through. My tears were no longer because I wished things could somehow be different. I cried because it was hard to say goodbye. I cried because I would miss our tea times and our cheesy movie nights. I cried because even though we had some hard moments that summer, we had shared some really good ones. With God's help, we were making it through those difficult teen and early adult years. We were figuring it out. We kept coming back to the table, and always will.

The Good, The Bad,
and the Eulogies

There is tremendous relief in knowing that His love to
me is utterly realistic, based at every point on prior
knowledge of the worst about me, so that no discovery
can disillusion him about me, in the way I am so often
disillusioned about myself, and quench his
determination to bless me.

—J.I. Packer, *Knowing God*

I think one of the most beautiful things about family is the
history we build together. We create a catalog, a series of
inside jokes and tales we tell and re-tell. For instance, our
amazing goldfish, Sparky, (whose adoption was forced upon
us when one of our daughters won him as a prize at Awana)
lived for more than five years! Or was it ten? We hardly ever
fed him or changed his water, and his resilience through
years of living in murky sludge was worth remembering and
even exaggerating. We remember vacations and holidays,
special milestones, and life-changing events. We remember
extraordinary things that happened on ordinary days. We
celebrate one another's accomplishments and make fun of
each other's quirks. We share experiences that create strong
bonds, some of them pleasant and some of them painful, but
they connect us in ways that last a lifetime. My parents
divorced many years ago, and I'm not in frequent contact
with all of my siblings, but when we do get together, we

inevitably start telling stories. Some of them I remember, and since I'm the fourth of five children some of the stories were before my time, but I'm always reminded that we are connected in a way no other people on the planet are. Even with all the brokenness in our family, these are *our* stories.

And when it comes to physical injuries and accidents, the crazier and bloodier the better. We love to retell stories about stitches and broken bones, about the time my brother drove our Suburban into a lake, and when I cracked my head open on Father's Day. My brothers were throwing the baseball in the backyard and my dad was grilling steaks on our stone fire pit. I was the designated ball fetcher, and when an overthrow rolled behind the swing set, I ran full speed to retrieve it. Up until that day I had been short enough to pass under the A-frame metal side of our swing set. I had done it a hundred times. But no one told me I'd gotten taller. No one warned, "Wow, Becky! You've had a growth spurt! Better not try to run under the swing set anymore. . . ." I can only imagine what it must have been like for my brothers to watch me run full force into that metal bar and split my forehead wide open. I only remember screaming and warm red running down my face. And then the "sting water" at the emergency room, and the way we all sat around the table a couple of hours—and several stitches—later for the delayed celebration supper. *Happy Father's Day, Dad.*

We do the same thing with our kids, reminiscing about the time Kate fell off her scooter and broke her wrist, but then refused to go to the emergency room until I gave her the Little Debbie snack cake I had promised her earlier that afternoon. Her determination and willingness to withstand significant discomfort shows how seriously our family takes dessert. And when Claire was four, she got knocked down by another kid at preschool, and though she kept saying she was fine, her mac and cheese was strangely too heavy for her to lift on her spoon at lunch. We were amazed a couple of hours later when the brilliant doctor at the emergency room performed the most amazing magic trick we had ever seen, sliding her elbow joint back in place as Claire reached out for a lollipop. The most traumatic injury award is a tie between when Claire slammed her finger in the door and when Brenna tripped on a step at a Pier One outlet store, knocking her front baby tooth completely up into her gum. Start telling those kinds of stories at a gathering and you'd better make yourself comfortable—you'll be there for hours!

We do not, however, always want to talk about the painful emotional wounds or hurts we've incurred in our families. We don't often want to talk about the dysfunction, destructive patterns, and family secrets. We avoid talking about things like abuse, betrayals, addictions, and suicide. We don't want to talk about bankruptcy and mental illness. For many of us, it can be really hard to tell the truth about our families.

After giving the eulogy at his mother's funeral, my friend Jan reflected on how we only share the positive memories of our loved ones after they die. We focus entirely on their most admirable qualities as we honor their memory along with our mutual loved ones. At the funeral, that is absolutely appropriate, but if we want to grieve in a way that leads to healing, we must find a way to be honest about the whole story. Jan's parents were missionaries when he was growing up, and he spent several years in boarding schools. He experienced a great deal of aloneness and neglect. There was pain and relational brokenness in his family that was never resolved, and the ripple effects of that brokenness continue to this day.

Shortly after his mom died, Jan opened up with our small group one evening, sharing some of his pain. He invited us to step into those spaces with him, and in the safety of our group, he was able to process both the good and the bad. God is a healer who loves to make his children whole in every way, and Jan was not the only one in our group who experienced healing as he shared his story.

Sometimes people say, "I don't need to dig up garbage from the past. Why would I want to dredge up old wounds and talk about all that negative stuff?" The purpose in talking about our wounds is not to blame others for our problems or complain about how hard we had it, but rather so we can be healed. We need to remember where we have come from and all we have weathered together because, for better and for worse, these things have shaped us. Whether we realize it fully or not, our past affects our present reality. And how we deal with our present reality affects our future.

I've learned that pain is an indicator, like a warning light on the dashboard of a car, alerting us that God wants to do his restorative work in us. Then, he wants to restore other people *through* us and our story. Something miraculous happens when we open our hearts and share our hurts with safe people. It's like having a friend hold our hand while a splinter is removed—it makes the telling of the pain bearable. When we open ourselves up to God's healing presence, he begins to bridge the gaps, often in the context of relationship with those who are walking with us. And as we are made whole, we are then able to see our loved one not only as the perpetrator of our pain, but as a person in need of a Savior. We see him or her as a flawed, wounded, precious human being. We can remember and love the whole person, the lovely parts as well as the broken parts. We can extend the grace we have so freely received.

All of us, moms included, are flawed and sinful humans. We all have been wounded, and we all inflict wounds on the people we love. I don't know who said it first, but it's true: hurt people hurt people. To the extent that we can be vulnerable and share our pain—to the extent that we can hold out our splintered hearts and allow God to do his redemptive work, we *can* be healed. We can break unhealthy patterns and learn how to love better.

At times, my temper still gets the best of me. Installing soft-close hinges on our kitchen cabinet doors has made it impossible for me to slam them, but there are still many ways for me to sin in my anger. I need God's help to not use my words as a weapon. I need my friends to help me understand what is driving my anger and what is fueling my intensity. I need the help of the Holy Spirit to produce fruit in keeping with repentance. My anger will never bring about the righteous life God desires or the loving, close relationships I desire. My kids know I am a work in progress. They know God is not done with me yet. I pray this realization gives them a context in which to view their own shortcomings. I pray this grace will color their worldview and enable them to love the way God does.

"But you, Lord, are a compassionate and gracious God, slow to anger, abounding in love and faithfulness" (Psalm 86:15).

Review:

While a mother's love is special and like no other, none of us are saints. We are all—moms included—flawed and sinful humans. We all have been wounded, and we all inflict wounds on the people we love. Only God's love is perfect and pure, and we need his help to love well.

Reflect:

1. Becky shared about her struggle with controlling anger and how it has impacted her daughters. What is a pattern of behavior you struggle with, and how is it affecting your relationships with your children (and others)? What steps can you take to change destructive patterns and move towards healing in your relationships?

2. Becky used the analogy that pain is like a warning light on the dashboard of a car, alerting us that God wants to heal us. What "warning lights" do you see on the dashboard of your life? Where might pain be acting as an indicator that God wants to heal you?

Respond:

God, thank you for your perfect love that drives out fear and sets me free. Help me to open my heart fully to your love for me so I can love my children the way you do. Let my motives in parenting be driven by your love instead of fears, insecurities, past wounds, and emotionally-charged responses. Help me to partner with you as I raise my children and not get in the way of what you are wanting to accomplish in my child's life. Amen.

#4—If Mama Ain't Happy, Ain't Nobody Happy

Climate Control

> Trying to control what I ultimately cannot
> will only make everyone (me included) miserable.
> —Shannon Popkin, *Control Girl*

I heard someone say it again the other day. "Moms are the barometer in the home." The first time I heard this concept was in a women's Bible study twenty years ago, and I have heard several variations of it over the years. *Moms set the tone for the whole family. Moms regulate the thermostat in the home.* The notion that "If mama ain't happy, ain't nobody happy" is closely related to its sister-saying, "Happy wife, happy life," and every time I hear either one of these I inwardly cringe. A barometer measures atmospheric pressure and is especially useful for predicting the weather. A thermostat automatically regulates temperature. The contrasting pictures these analogies paint in my head are of a mother who, because she is an emotional being, sets everyone around her off by her intense and sometimes negative feelings. She is a proverbial ticking time bomb—especially if she is ovulating, pregnant, breastfeeding, or experiencing premenstrual, perimenopausal, or menopausal symptoms—causing those around her to duck for cover as they yell, "Watch out . . . she's gonna blow!" Or, she is miraculously able to regulate the moods of everyone around her because of her incredible emotional and mental stability. No one ever feels even the slightest hint of a storm or a wave because she is maintaining perfect order and calm.

But this idea that mothers control the emotional climate in the home is a half-truth. An angry father returning from work can send everyone running for cover. A moody teenager can turn family dinner into an unpleasant time of togetherness, making everyone at the table want to scarf down their food as quickly as possible, just so it can be over. And an emotionally explosive toddler can put the kibosh on just about anything. Yelling and out-of-control anger—no matter who it's coming from—creates anxiety and chaos, and steely cold silence can be suffocating. Emotions are powerful and often messy, and we get into trouble when we try to deny our own or control someone else's.

As a mom, I know my attitude and tone create a ripple effect on my husband and children. And I can see how tension between my husband and me trickles down to our children. They sense when things are not OK. Yet trying to control the emotional climate in my home and assuming responsibility for the relational wellness of every member in my family does not produce what I am so desperately trying to accomplish. I want peace, harmony, and intimacy; what I get is frustration, depletion, and burn out. Moms can't make everyone happy by being happy. Moms get sad, angry, and scared and need space to express their humanness. Each family member must learn to take responsibility for his or her own emotions and responses, without blaming or trying to control others.

Moms who struggle with depression and anxiety often feel the added burden of needing to hide their struggles from their families. My nieces, Rachel and Emily, used to come visit us regularly when they were growing up, along with their sister, Sarah. Now they are all married with children, and Rachel and Emily have allowed me to share their thoughts about their struggles with depression and anxiety. They hope that other moms will be encouraged and know they are not alone.

> Parenting through depression is a daily battle. It's the cycle of, I know my kids need to eat but I can't even get out of bed, leading to, I'm such a failure as a parent—I'm never going to be good enough. My kids deserve a mom who isn't depressed. Which makes it even harder to get out of bed. This is especially difficult when the church's response is, "Pray more, read your Bible more." Basically, you're not a good enough Christian in addition to not being a good enough mom.

While I haven't experienced the kind of chronic, persistent, and biochemical depression Rachel and Emily are talking about, after my mom died, I went through a deep period of grieving. I did the hard work of feeling my feelings rather than numbing the pain, which meant that my sadness was front and center for many months following her death. It would have been hard for me to hide my grief from my children even if I had tried, and I believed there was value in letting them see my process. I wanted them to know that sadness isn't something we need to cover up or hide. It is a response to loss, and we will not experience comfort if we do not grieve.

One day, I was having some quiet time in our living room, writing in my journal, letting my tears flow freely down my cheeks. Brenna, who was eight years old, came up to me and handed me a note she had written. It said, "Mommy, I love to see you cry because it shows me your beautiful heart." I didn't know she was watching me that morning. If I had, I may have tried to temper my tears a bit. But seeing my tears did not make Brenna sad or distressed. It showed her my heart and gave her an opportunity to love and comfort me. It created an opportunity for connection with my child. Rachel and Emily believe it's important that, as moms, we shift our mindset when it comes to letting our children see our struggles.

It's OK that our kids see us sad, because one day they will be super sad too. They will know how to manage it and how to reach out for help. Hopefully they will realize it is not an emotion that has to be hidden. They'll also know how to treat someone with depression or other mental health problems.

When Rachel is having a hard day, her eight-year-old daughter Alexis will draw her a card and say, "I think you are feeling sad today, so I made you a card and I'll rub your back." Her son Lucas, who is eleven, will give her a hug and sit by her. Both of them know that sometimes she will want to talk about how she is feeling, but most of the time, them just being there makes the biggest difference. Rachel shares,

It honestly makes me proud—when I can forget my guilt over them deserving better— because I have a feeling when they get to high school, college, or beyond they'll know how to spot someone who is struggling. And they'll know how to respond. They will be there for others who are hurting whether they need to talk or not. So many people with mental health issues go unnoticed. But I think my kids will notice. If nothing else, I have taught them to be real, that it's ok to be real, and how to respond to real.

One day Emily—who had already had a tough week— texted Rachel a video of her son, Spencer, who was almost three. It was just after dinner, and Emily was curled up with a blanket on the couch, still in her pajamas from the previous night. Spencer wanted to play hide-and-seek, but she just couldn't muster the energy or desire to get up and play. So she stayed on the couch and counted slowly to ten while Spencer ran away, somewhere off camera. When she got to ten, she yelled, "Ready or not, come on out!" and Spencer came running back, giggling, with a giant smile on his face. They did that over and over for at least 15 minutes. Emily sent the video with the caption, "Just because I'm depressed doesn't make me a bad mom." She was a perfect example of adjusting expectations to help mitigate the effects of depression and mom guilt. She's still a great mom—it just looks different.

This story illustrates the truth that even if Mama ain't happy, we can still all be okay. We can still be together and find moments of joy as we love each other right where we are. With God's help, we can move from shame to a place of acceptance. We do not have to stay stuck in the defeat of thinking our kids deserve a mom who isn't depressed. Instead, we can embrace the beautiful, healing truth that our kids want us even when we aren't happy. They love us even when we are sad. And God is with us, even when we feel like we are failing at every turn.

Broken Parenting

It is in families that we are broken, and it is in families
that we are healed.

—Carl Whitaker

We all parent out of our brokenness. Our parents did too.
Like a baton that is handed down from generation to
generation, we take what we are given and run with it. Our
baton may be in pretty good shape, showing small
imperfections and minor signs of wear and tear. Or it may be
rusty, cracked, or broken in half and repaired with duct
tape—we don't get to choose the condition of the baton we
are given. Sometimes we unknowingly repeat unhealthy
patterns from our own families of origin. Other times, even
though we are aware and desire to break these patterns, we
feel powerless to change and do things differently. Or, we
may identify dysfunctional behaviors and vow not to repeat
them, but then overcompensate in other ways. We may
become overprotective, always looking to shield our children
from pain. We may work to provide not only all of our
children's needs, but all of their wants as well, so they don't
feel the lack we felt growing up. We may inadvertently
project our own grief, fears, and insecurities onto our
children, or choose not to push them to excel at anything,
because we were pushed too hard when we were kids.

While we can't control the condition of the batons we are
given, we decide everyday what to do with the broken pieces
in our lives. Whether we are aware of it or not, we are always
moving in one of two directions: towards perpetuating our

brokenness or towards healing. We can choose to ignore and numb the pain, blame others for our mistakes, make excuses for our behavior, or live as a victim to our circumstances. Or, we can take our broken pieces to God and seek healing. His healing may come as a direct, supernatural touch as we pour out our hurts to him, but more often I have found that he chooses to heal in the context of relationship. He loves to bring healing *to* his people *through* his people. We open up with a trusted friend who listens, empathizes, and prays with us. We are inspired by a speaker who shares her story. We read a book that causes hope to come alive inside us. We attend a workshop and learn about the process of growth. We listen as a gifted teacher opens God's Word and shares truth that transforms us from the inside out. We seek the help of a therapist who guides and supports us as we unpack the most wounded parts of our stories. We seek help from skilled doctors who use medicine to treat ailments in our bodies and chemical imbalances in our brains.

When I was a child, I experienced an incident of abuse by an acquaintance who stayed in our home, and I thought I had dealt with it. I thought it had been wrapped up and tucked away forever. I thought it was dead and powerless, so I buried it deep inside of me. For many years, I wouldn't even allow myself to think about what had happened, and the few people in whom I confided knew very few details. I was surprised when, in my forties, I began to have flashbacks of the incident. It started showing up in my dreams. My youngest daughter was about the age I had been when the abuse occurred, and something about seeing her at that age triggered this wound in me that had been dormant for more than three decades. Unresolved pain surfaced in my life, and no matter how hard I tried to push it back down, it kept coming back up. It was seeping into my relationships; it was impacting my marriage and parenting.

At the advice of a friend, I decided to see a counselor. As I was walking out to my car after my first session, I remember thinking, *What have I done? I just opened up a trapdoor, unearthing enough pain and shame to swallow me up. Isn't this the reason why we bury these kinds of things? Because we fear they will swallow us whole and destroy us? I don't think I will ever be OK again.*

In the days following that first appointment, as I grappled with the ramifications of having opened that old wound, the same thoughts kept coming to mind. *God is a healer and he loves me. The only reason he would allow this pain from my past to resurface at this time in my life is that he wants to heal me.*

My counselor was gentle and compassionate in the months that followed. She helped me process what happened and reframe some of the conclusions I had drawn from that experience: conclusions about myself, and conclusions about God. I shared pieces of my story—not every detail—and as I did, the healing came. I could not have done this work on my own. I allowed God to work through my counselor, clinging to the hope that he would lead me to a better place.

If we view the pain from our past as an indicator that God wants to heal us, our perspective in parenting shifts. Our struggles, shortcomings, and patterns that we feel powerless to change can usher in the transforming grace of God, and our kids get to witness it. We are works in progress, every one of us, and it is more than OK to let our kids know it. As we lean into and become aware of our brokenness, and our tendencies to parent out of it, we open the door to healing and change. As we recognize and name the anxiety, depression, addictions, abuse, anger, guilt, and shame, we normalize our struggles instead of hiding them or pretending they don't exist. And as we learn to live authentically in front of our children, with our hearts in an ongoing process of being restored, the most beautiful thing happens. Our children receive a mended, transformed baton. They receive tools, knowledge, understanding, wisdom, skills, stories of redemption and faith, and an updated family history. Then they will take their imperfect, not-yet-completely-whole batons and run with them. And we will watch and cheer them on as God does it all over again.

Mom Guilt

Behind every great kid is a mom
who's pretty sure she's screwing it all up.
—author unknown

One day my friend, Tricia, was waiting outside the school to pick up her son Jack from first grade. When she heard one of the other moms talking about how excited her daughter had been to bring her mermaid blanket to school for Super Reader Day, Tricia's heart sank. Covering her face with her hands, she told her friend that she had forgotten all about it. She had received numerous emails about the special day, but had forgotten that morning to send Jack with his special blanket, stuffed animal, and favorite book to read. Feeling mortified, she imagined how disappointed Jack must have felt when he opened his backpack and realized he didn't have the special things he needed for Super Reader Day. Why hadn't she set a reminder on her phone? When Jack came out of school, he seemed fine. She was surprised that he wasn't visibly upset and asked him to tell her about Super Reader Day. He admitted he felt worried and confused when he opened his backpack and didn't see his blanket, stuffed animal, and favorite book. Normally he had what he needed in his backpack. So he went to his teacher and asked what he should do. She said he could choose a stuffed animal from the extras she had brought in a bag, and then invited him to choose a book to read from her book box. Then he took his borrowed items, settled into a spot on the gym floor, and read along with the other children. Feeling terrible, Tricia said, "I'm so sorry I forgot." Jack looked up at her and said, "It's OK, Mom—I forgive you."

When Tricia told me this story, I did what we often do: I told her about a time I messed up to try to make her feel better. I told her about how I forgot to pick up my sixth-grader from school—twice in one week! And then, for good measure, I told her about my sister, Kari, who once sent three of her five kids to school in their pajamas for Pajama Day. The principal was going to read a book to the entire school in the gym, and the kids were supposed to bring their pillows and a blanket. This was news to the older kids who hadn't heard anything about a school-wide Pajama Day, but they did as they were told. When she picked them up after school that day, Kari discovered that it had only been Pajama Day for the *youngest* child. The older kids had to go through their day in their pajamas, with their blankets and pillows in tow.

What struck me most about Tricia's story was Jack's resilience. Sure, he was disappointed, but the fact that his mom made a mistake and forgot to send him to school with his special items did not derail him. It didn't wreck his whole day. He knew how to ask for help, and he was able to be flexible, adjust his expectations, and still enjoy Super Reader Day. Then he was able to be gracious towards his mom while being honest about his disappointment. Tricia realized through that incident that she needed to be better about marking her calendar so she didn't forget important events. They both were able to move on and grow from that experience.

When I asked moms on social media to tell me about their mom guilt, I thought I'd get a lot of comments and start a dialogue about this topic that affects every mom I know. But instead of comments and conversation, my inbox was flooded with personal messages. Many moms wanted to share, but they didn't want to do it publicly. They didn't want their names put out there. I discovered that lots of moms are feeling guilt over similar things—often things completely out of their control—and for many moms, the guilt over their perceived shortcomings has turned into deep-rooted shame and a pervasive sense of failure. The progression from guilt to shame is sneaky and nuanced. Guilt says, *I should have done that better.* Shame says, *I should be better.* Guilt says, *I hurt my kids when I lost my temper.* Shame says, *My kids deserve better than to have a mom like me.*

Following are actual messages I received from moms in various stages of motherhood who had a lot to say about guilt and shame:

The guilt from all the things you could and should be doing weighs heavily on an already crushed mental status. It feels quite hopeless. Then, when you muster up the energy to do something fun with the kids and it doesn't turn out right, or they don't react the way you expect them too, it's even worse. Because you failed. And you don't know when you'll have the energy to try again.

When my child has a tantrum, it's my fault because I have been too harsh, or not harsh enough—bottom line, I'm not a good enough parent. When my kid doesn't like dinner, I'm not good enough to meet her needs because I should have tried harder to introduce new foods, should have presented it in a pretty manner or something . . . anything would be better than what I did.

I'm having major mom guilt right now about the likelihood that we won't be giving our daughter a sibling and how that will affect the rest of her life. . . .

If you work, there's guilt for being away. If you stay at home, there's guilt for not making money and contributing financially so they can have great vacations, new toys or clothes, or the latest extracurricular activity.

If my child gets sick, I didn't clean my house well enough, wash their hands enough, or do enough to protect them. It's a constant cycle of not being enough. It can feel very hopeless and overwhelming. For someone with depression—like me—it can be crushing.

One mom messaged me and shared about her experience that very morning.

My three-and-a-half-year-old son is a challenge. It took everything out of me to get him in the car for a doctor's appointment this morning. I yelled. I threatened to take away toys. I even said, "What is wrong with you?" which I know is so awful. How could I say that to someone I love so much and is so young? What is wrong with him? He doesn't want to go to the doctor, that's what. He is scared. In the moment my anxiety took over as I was looking at the clock, seeing we only have so much time to get there. My fear of being late consumed me. My almost three-month-old also began to cry in her car seat, and I had no patience. My overwhelming guilt of how I treated my little boy who is just scared is eating away at me. Yes, he has tantrums and doesn't like to listen most of the time, but rather than finding patience, I let anxiety fill me instead. I cried in the car on the way to the doctor appointment and reached back to hold his hands, apologizing and telling him I love him.

I often feel guilty when we go through his tantrums and situations where I feel like I have to physically get him in the car or to his room or off the floor of a store. It's easy to feel guilty other times too. I get anxious over a mess, and with three children, a mess is constant. Most nights, I look back on the day and think I should have played more, read more, or held them more rather than focused so much on trying to clean. I need to learn to let some of that anxiety about time and the mess go, and just be in the moment.

Another mom shared,

I have definitely had guilt and shame for the past four years since my oldest was born, and I have had anxiety and depression as long as I can remember. I finally feel like I am more in control of my anxiety, because I know God has me. But my guilt has usually been over not being able to accomplish the idea of how I thought something was supposed to be. So if I thought the kids were supposed to sleep through the night and they didn't, it was because I was doing everything wrong. Or, other parts of my life weren't where they "should be," which meant that I couldn't devote enough time or effort to really fix the problem of the kids not sleeping. Looking back, I realize that my thoughts of failure stemmed from the expectations of "what should be" according to baby books, Google, friends or family member's advice, and comparing myself to others on social media. Now I know those were lies. But when I was— and am—in it, it all feels so real.

Once I began to realize that God loves me no matter if I accomplish any of the things I am "supposed" to accomplish, I have been able to focus on one thing at a time, turn off the lies, and choose what matters most to me.

A mom who is now an empty nester shared her long-standing guilt:

After thinking about it, I realized my mom guilt came from having three miscarriages, some failed half-hearted adoption attempts, and then finally giving up on providing a sibling for my son. We were tired of the grief and the roller coaster ride of emotions . . . I wish I had persevered.

So, not only does he not have any siblings, but his kids won't have any cousins on our side and our family always seems small. My mom guilt comes from putting too much control/attention/focus on him because he's my only one, and I had a lot of mom energy. By senior year, he pushed hard for independence, and I was anxious about safety issues. I turned things over to my husband, and I had to back off.

My mom guilt surfaces with my severe empty nest syndrome issues. I have had to grieve through that and practice letting go and backing off for years. I am thankful for the group of moms who have helped me with that. So, the mom guilt is here, just in a unique way. I know I tried to do my best, but it wasn't a perfect ride. I know God forgives me for all of it, and He makes up for what I couldn't give.

Another mom in the empty nest years shared,

I am trying to learn to be a mom of a married child, and it's even worse than being an empty nester! It's a whole new relationship with my daughter now, and it's distant. I don't like that, and don't know how to fix it or even if I should try to fix it. It's definitely an adjustment that I obviously am not handling well.

As you can see—for many of us—mom guilt begins the moment we become mothers and can continue well into our children's adult years. After losing my first baby three months into my pregnancy, I was racked with guilt over what I must have done to cause my miscarriage. It must have been the sweetener I used before knowing I was pregnant, or some physical activity I did that triggered a problem. I asked my doctor repeatedly what I had done to cause it, and finally she said, "Becky, we have talked about this many times. You have asked me this question a dozen different ways. This was not your fault. Nothing you did caused it, and nothing you could have done would have prevented it. You have to let this go."

Over the years, I've felt guilty when my kids have gotten sick, when they bring up things I didn't let them do during their childhoods (I didn't know my eldest daughter's deepest longing as a child was to play the saxophone), when they've judged me as being unfair, and when we've had to say no to things they really wanted. I've felt guilty because I only volunteered to be a room mom once in seventeen years of schooling, and I was terrible at it. I've felt guilty for saying no to sleepovers at our house because we don't have a basement, and for losing my temper about a million times over the last 21 years with my kids.

Where does all this guilt and shame come from, and more importantly, what do we do with it? My friend, Beth, (who I met in college) and her husband, Brad, lived in South Africa for 18 years and currently reside in Wisconsin. Their five children—four biological sons and one adopted daughter—have had both homeschooling and traditional classroom experiences. Beth shared her thoughts on these questions, and her insights are profound.

With the amount of information available to us in any given moment, we are inundated with ideas about how to mother. "You should feed your children in this way. You should discipline your children in this way. You should educate them in this way. You should raise them like this . . ." I have found this mentality particularly pervasive in the homeschooling circles. Because we have chosen to closely guide our children's education (as in, doing it ourselves), there is an unbelievably heavy burden of responsibility that rests on our shoulders. (I do not write that to in any way lesson the burden that non-homeschooling mothers experience—it is simply part of my journey.)

So where does the guilt come in? I believe much of it comes through my desire to do things perfectly and the failure to meet someone else's standard. And how do we measure failure? In my case, I have been guilty of measuring it through comparison. How are my children doing when I hold them up next to yours? This is such a deceptive practice to adopt. How do I really know how your kids are doing? Well, they have accomplished this and that (according to social media or comments that might be shared with me personally) and mine haven't. Enter failure. Enter guilt.

The season where I have felt the most guilt is the one I am currently in. I have known guilt along the parenting journey, but nothing prepared me for the helpless feeling and overwhelming regret I would feel as my children came to an age to leave home. Have I done enough? Have I enjoyed every moment? Have I prepared them for what is to come? And the myriad questions that follow fill me with guilt.

With the help of her counselor Beth has come to understand that she has an overdeveloped sense of responsibility that is rooted in her childhood. Family situations pushed her to take on adult responsibilities while not yet an adult, which set her up to feel even much more guilt in her parenting journey. The hard work she has done in therapy has brought new awareness, and her friendships have also been a great support and help. When she feels overwhelmed with guilt or regrets and takes her grief to God, he brings clarity and comfort. She is finding healing and a path forward as she strives to live in increasing freedom from guilt and shame. She writes,

I am beginning to see how many areas I have felt responsible for in my children's lives that are not mine to carry. It is a process of learning to let go of those areas and lean fully into Christ. How I thought that I was better able to carry those myself is beyond me and was a serious deception that I am choosing to walk away from. I recognize my need to continually "take every thought captive" as the heavy feelings of regret, shame, and guilt threaten to consume me time and again.

As I have begun to let go of these burdens, I find that the freedom I receive in exchange actually empowers me to mother in a more effective way than before. Why am I surprised? The Scriptures are full of directives to cast our cares, walk by faith, and trust in the Lord. Thinking that I could accomplish things that have always been God's work probably originates in a legalistic, works-based mindset that makes self an idol. Thinking this is all up to me, instead of trusting the One who made my children and knows and loves them far beyond my understanding, only leads to bondage.

In conclusion, guilt should serve the same purpose that pain does. It should make us stop and ask ourselves, "Why am I feeling this? What do I need to see about myself? Is this the Holy Spirit convicting me of something I need to repent of, or is this the enemy whispering his poisonous condemnation into my mind? What is God wanting to show me through this? Where is He wanting to bring freedom?" How I answer these questions can determine how I move forward and whether or not I can walk away from the grasp of guilt.

These are wise words for weary moms. Perfectionism, comparison, guilt, and unrealistic expectations are like heavy, back-breaking burdens we were never meant to carry. Should we repent and ask forgiveness when we miss the mark? Absolutely. Should we keep pursuing growth and healing? Always! But there is something else Jesus invites us to do, especially if we are worn out from our own sense of failure and regret and exhausted from trying to do it all perfectly.

Are you tired? Worn out? Burned out on religion? Come to me. Get away with me and you'll recover your life. I'll show you how to take a real rest. Walk with me and work with me—watch how I do it. Learn the unforced rhythms of grace. I won't lay anything heavy or ill-fitting on you. Keep company with me and you'll learn to live freely and lightly. (Matthew 11:28-30, THE MESSAGE)

These "unforced rhythms of grace" hint at a back-and-forth movement. In the many times we miss the mark, acknowledge our failures, and ask for forgiveness; in our resolution to keep moving forward; in our determination to shed the guilt and shame that weigh us down, and instead, live in the truth that we are forgiven, our children are watching. They are taking notes. As we submit ourselves to the transforming work of the Holy Spirit, our children experience these rhythms of grace right alongside us. It is hands-on learning at its best. Our most despised weaknesses can become tools God uses to shape our children. He can use our mistakes to equip them for times they will be disappointed by others. He uses our shortcomings to teach them how to forgive. As we model humility with our children, he teaches them how to be gracious and compassionate. He uses our mishaps and oversights to help them become flexible humans who are capable of problem solving. He uses our forgetfulness to remind our children that they don't have to fall apart when things are not perfect, because he is their ever-present help.

In the terrible realization that we cannot be the perfect mothers we would like to be, there are some equally staggering, magnificent truths: He is everything we are not. He measures up where we fall short. His strength is made perfect in our weakness. Like brilliant stars spread across a night sky, his absolute perfection and faithfulness shine most brightly in contrast to our imperfections and flaws. Moms, it's time to lay down our heavy burdens of perfectionism and shame. Jesus is inviting us to pick up his light, made-for-us yoke—his freedom-filled provision of grace. We don't have to keep striving. We can live freely and lightly. For the first time in a long time—maybe as long as we can remember—we can find real rest in him.

Review:

We are always moving in one of two directions: towards perpetuating our brokenness or towards healing. If we view emotional pain as an indicator that God wants to heal us, our perspective in parenting shifts. The struggles, shortcomings, and patterns we feel powerless to change can usher in the transforming grace of God, and our kids get to witness it. We don't have to hide our struggles or pretend they don't exist. As we live authentically in front of our children, with our hearts in an ongoing process of being restored, our children receive a mended, transformed baton.

Reflect:

1. In what condition was the "baton" you received from your first family?

2. In what ways might you be perpetuating the brokenness in your life, and how can you move towards healing?

3. In what areas do you most often experience mom guilt? How can you begin to move away from shame-based guilt that does not bring about change, and instead receive God's grace when you fall short, live in the truth that you are forgiven and loved, and find real rest in Jesus?

Respond:

You have searched me, Lord,
  and you know me.
You know when I sit and when I rise;
  you perceive my thoughts from afar.
You discern my going out and my lying down;
  you are familiar with all my ways.
Before a word is on my tongue
  you, Lord, know it completely. . . .
Where can I go from your Spirit?
  Where can I flee from your presence?
If I go up to the heavens, you are there;
  if I make my bed in the depths, you are there.

(Psalm 139:1-4, 7-8)

God, you know me inside and out. Heal the brokenness in
my life so I may be whole. Thank you for loving me just as I
am. Amen.

#5—Just Wait Until They Become Teenagers!

Pushing My Panic Buttons

*When your children are teenagers, it's important to
have a dog so that someone in the house
is happy to see you.*
—Nora Ephron

In chapter one, I told the story of meeting a woman in an elevator one day when my two older daughters were preschoolers. This woman was probably sixty years old, and when she saw the girls sitting very nicely in their double stroller she exclaimed, "Oh, it's *sooo* easy when they are little like that! They listen to everything you say!" But that's not all. She had one final zinger to throw out before heading on her way. As she stepped off the elevator, she looked over her shoulder and quipped, "Just wait till they become teenagers!"

It was not the first time I had heard some verbal warning from a jaded onlooker. I tucked her comment away in my mental file cabinet where I had been storing other similar comments for years—ones that filled my husband and me with fear and dread. When we were newly married, we heard, "Oh, you are so in love right now, just wait till you have kids and you've been married for ten years!" People told us, "The first year of marriage is the hardest." Not ours—we had an extended honeymoon period for the first few years. When our babies were born, people warned, "Just wait till you hit the Terrible Twos!" Personally, I thought the Horrible Threes were worse. Then we heard about the marital "seven-year itch" which actually *was* a hard year for us. Bernie's parents visited us during that year, and when they saw how much we were struggling in our marriage, my mother-in-law (who is Mexican) asked how long we had been married. I told her seven years, and she replied, "Ah, es el año de la crisis!" which means, "it's the year of crisis." Actually, years five through ten were quite "itchy" and crisis-laden in our marriage. And when people notice we have three daughters, often they look directly at Bernie and said, "Wow! Three weddings? Better get another job!"

Comments like these are usually made in innocent jest with no regard for the ensuing panic parents often experience. I used to tell my former co-worker (who is also a good friend) about all kinds of stressful situations with my kids, and she would often remind me of how much worse it was going to get. I'd complain about tight finances and she'd say, "You think it's bad now, just wait till they're in college! You will never be richer than you are right now." *Huh? Is that supposed to make me feel better?*

Three of my sister's five children are now teenagers, and she has been dreading this current stage of parenting for years, because so many people have warned her about how awful it's going to be. When I told her I was going to write this chapter, she said, "Please give moms like me hope that this season of motherhood isn't all bad. Speak words of positivity and tell us how we can enjoy this stage. Help us see the best things about these years, and remind us to have fun and enjoy who our kids are becoming."

Let's begin by breaking this panic-inducing sentence down, shall we? One misconception implied in "Just wait until they become teenagers!" is that our children suddenly become teenagers overnight. I mean, technically that is true. On the day of his or her thirteenth birthday, a child officially becomes a teenager. But this idea that all of a sudden we are going to be dealing with some version of our child whom we do not recognize, that is just . . . well, that is also kind of true. It probably won't happen exactly on the day of their thirteenth birthdays, but it can seem like our sweet children become unrecognizable to us within a short period of time upon entering adolescence. So before we get to the hope and positivity, let's start by being honest about the challenges of raising teens. Though every stage of parenting has its challenges, there are reasons why many people single out the teen years as the hardest.

In his book, *Boundaries with Teens*, Dr. John Townsend addresses the challenges parents often face during the teen years. He describes an adolescent as someone who possibly:

- has a disrespectful attitude toward parents, family, and others
- challenges requests or rules
- is self-absorbed and unable to see things from anyone else's perspective
- is lazy and careless about responsibilities
- is emotionally withdrawn and distant from you
- has mood shifts that seem to have neither rhyme nor reason
- lacks interest in spiritual matters
- detaches from family events and wants to be with friends only
- lies and is deceptive about activities
- is physically aggressive and violent
- abuses substances—alcohol, drugs, pornography
- engages in sexual activity [2]

If you are the parent of a teenager and are experiencing some of these struggles, you may feel relieved to know that you are not alone. These behaviors are common enough that they made it into Townsend's book about parenting teens. Or maybe you feel grateful that, though your teens can be difficult, they are not engaging in some of the riskier, more destructive behaviors mentioned on this list.

If you are the parent of a young child, this list may shock you. You may think, *Oh, my sweet child will never act out in these ways.* Maybe you're thinking that if you step up your game and just do better, you can prevent your child from turning into the juvenile delinquent described on this list. Or maybe, at this point, you want to throw this book across the room because, in sharing this information with you I have effectively validated the warning I am trying to challenge. Maybe your fears are heightened now that you've read some of the reasons that cause parents to say, "Just wait till they are teenagers!"

Here is what is true: When you do get to the teenage years, your child will not suddenly become all bad and you will not suddenly become a parent who has no idea how to handle difficult situations. Each stage of parenting progresses into the next, which means that by the time your child reaches his or her teen years, you will have already been dealing with some problematic behaviors that needed to be addressed. Parenting teens is challenging, but so are other stages of parenthood. Some babies cry all the time and don't let their parents sleep for two years. Some children are so strong-willed they turn everything into a battle. Some kids are especially challenging in middle school and then calm down in high school. And all teenagers are not the same degree of difficult. You have made it through the hard stuff of other seasons, and *you will make it through these years.* You taught your preschooler that the world did not revolve around her, which means you are qualified to teach the level 201 version of that same class to your teenager. You taught your toddler there are consequences for disobeying, and you can do it again with your teen. Instead of a time out, he gets his phone or the car taken away. You will still be the same mother, and your child will still be your child.

Many of us read *What to Expect When You Are Expecting* before we even became mothers. Then we read books on sleep and potty training, discipline, and how to discover our child's love language. We've been educating ourselves for years, growing and learning right alongside our children, and so we continue. We keep adding to the knowledge we have already acquired and get some additional books for our nightstand during the teen years. We keep asking God for wisdom (James 1:5). We continue to rely on our friends, learning from those who are further along on this journey, as well as those who are in the same season as us and facing similar challenges. And when we feel like we are in over our heads, there are other kinds of resources, too. There is help—for us and for our kids. We may need experienced counselors we can turn to for advice and help when working through a particularly difficult issue. We may need to find a good support group and connect with other parents who are going through something similar. And our kids may need to talk to a professional. It is not a sign of weakness for your child to need the help of a doctor or therapist. On the contrary, one of the best things we can do as parents is to teach our children how to ask for help when they need it. Recently, a friend and I were practically giving each other high fives because all of our college-aged children have found good therapists. We don't see this as a failure on our part that our kids need help: we see it as a positive and healthy sign that they recognize their need for support and know where to go to get it.

Parenting my daughters through their teen years has been challenging for me in several ways. Dealing with mood swings, disrespectful attitudes, dishonesty, boyfriends and breakups, and emotional distancing has been hard. At times they haven't wanted to come to family dinner or attend church, choosing instead to spend almost all their time in their rooms. I've wondered how hard I should push my teen to interact when they don't feel like it, and no matter how I try to handle a difficult situation, there is usually a pervasive sense of "not getting it right."

And then there are the maddeningly irritating behaviors that have the potential to push moms to the brink of insanity. *Why do they have so many water bottles? And why must they leave them in every room of the house? How come no one replaces the empty toilet paper roll? And where is all of our missing silverware?* Seriously, I lost half of my spoons and all but one of my salad forks in a period of a year and a half. Harder still was watching them back our car out of the garage and drive away for the first time, and the many late nights waiting for them to get home. Letting go is *hard*. The inevitable pulling away that happens during these years has often felt like rejection to me. I have worked hard as a mom from the time my daughters were little to develop close, connected relationships, and it has been very painful when those connections have felt distant or strained.

But now . . . let me tell you what I *love* about this age. I love that we are getting to see our children become adults right before our eyes. I love that we get a front row seat as they discover their passions and step into leadership roles. I am blown away by their wisdom in moments when I don't expect it, and the deep—sometimes hard—questions they ask. I love the occasional moments when they see and appreciate all we do and who we are as parents. It's exciting to see them get their first jobs, discover their gifts, work through hardships, and move towards independence. And I love their friends. I love the community they create and the way they show up for one another.

I also love their humor, even when it's at my expense. One day, I told Claire that I felt like a pioneer woman because I was making homemade bread (from a mix), and she said, "Oh, like you make "homemade" Ranch dressing from a packet?" I was pleased to see that she had inherited my gift of sarcasm. And I love the way my daughters form alliances with one another. A few years back, I got tired of hearing Kate (15) and Claire (13) call each other stupid. They insisted they were just joking, but I didn't like it. So, I told them that from that point forward, every time they called each other stupid they would have to pay me a dollar. *Good parenting, Becky.*

Kate had a suggestion. "Well, how about if instead of paying *you* a dollar, we have to pay *each other* a dollar?"

"Ohhh . . . good idea, Kate! OK, we agree then—if you call each other stupid you have to pay each other one dollar."

Both girls agreed. Almost immediately, Claire said, "Stupid!"

To which Kate replied, "Stupid!"

Then both girls in unison: "We're even!"

I guess it wasn't great parenting after all, but it sure made me laugh. This is one of my favorite memories of those years (which were often wrought with stress and chaos) because it gave me a glimpse of not just their brilliant humor, but of the relationship they were forging as sisters. The girls call it "proper banter," and I've seen them develop this not just as sisters, but also with their cousins, their friends, and with us as parents. Connecting through humor is one of the best ways to enjoy your teen.

My friend, Scott, has been a youth pastor for twenty years, and he and his wife have raised three teen boys of their own. I asked him if he could tell me a couple of his favorite things about working with teens and his email began with the words, "SO many things..." If you've been waiting for the hope and positivity, here it is:

- They have PASSION.
- They ask probing questions, and if they know you're truly taking them seriously, they'll share their thoughts and opinions. Sometimes, they may even ask for yours.

- They have HALF A CENTURY or more of life in front of them, and so anything they discover as a teenager literally has DECADES to grow and bear fruit.
- They don't take things at face value.
- They believe they can change the world, because they've (usually) not been beaten down by life yet.
- When someone believes in them, they can take courageous and bold steps that lots of adults would be terrified by.
- They can simultaneously be both naive and wise-beyond-their-years.
- They are on the lookout for love.
- When Jesus takes hold of their life LITERALLY ANYTHING can happen.
- They will usually forgive when an adult humbly apologizes.
- While we are trying to "impact" them, they actually have the power to impact us beyond what we ever imagined.
- They grow up, and SOME of them still remember what it was like to be a teenager—and the ones who do can turn around and breathe belief into the next generation of teenagers.

The teen years can, indeed, be challenging, but that is not all. When we tell younger moms, "Just wait till they become teenagers!" let's make sure we tell them the whole story. Let's give them the good news along with the hard, and the hope along with the warning. Let's remind them they have been training for these years all their parenting lives. And most importantly, let's encourage them that they don't have to do it alone. There are friends who are a phone call away, aunts and uncles, grandparents who may know a thing or two about raising teens, books and support groups, classes and youth group leaders, doctors and therapists, and the ever-present help of our God. He promises to give wisdom when we don't know what to do, and strength when we are weary.

He didn't bring us this far to leave us. ". . . Being confident of this, that he who began a good work in you will carry it on to completion until the day of Christ Jesus" (Philippians 1:6).

Q-tips and Parenting

Be brave enough to start a conversation that matters.
—Margaret Wheatley

I was surprised when I noticed my Q-tip box has pictures and recommendations for all sort of uses—such as applying ointments, cleaning the grout in your shower, and dusting your computer keyboard—except the most obvious one: cleaning your ears. Every year, thousands of people—mostly children—end up in the ER with Q-tip related injuries.[3] Yet, aside from a small warning printed on the side of the box (which I could not even find until a friend pointed it out), it is not clearly addressed. It's as if the Q-tip people do not want to give us any ideas; maybe if they pretend that consumers are not sticking this product in their ears, there won't be any problems.

We do the same thing in parenting. How often do we avoid talking to our kids about certain topics because we feel uncomfortable, awkward, or embarrassed? How often do we skirt around an issue with our teenager, avoiding the elephant in the room? We may drop subtle hints, use non-verbal body language, or even use sarcasm to try to make our point. Sometimes these cues are received and understood, but more often they are like small letters on the side of a box: easy to miss. We avoid talking about difficult subjects like sexual behaviors, drug and alcohol use, self-image issues, addictions, depression, and anxiety. We steer clear of hard conversations because we do not want to create conflict. We choose to not bring up possible pitfalls our kids may encounter because we don't want to "put ideas in their heads." Too frequently we give our attention to the temporal, insignificant details in our lives while overlooking things that are eternally significant. Although it can be so hard to do, we must be intentional to give honest, direct communication a prominent place in our parenting.

The best advice I've received about when to talk to my kids about sex came from my niece, Rachel. She was in her early twenties and living with us at the time. I asked her whether she thought my daughter (who was a bright and inquisitive eight-year-old) was too young for me to bring up certain topics of sexuality. Rachel's wise-beyond-her-years answer blew me away. She said, "You can wait and let her hear about all these things at school—and she *is* hearing about them—and then try and correct, explain, and fill in the gaps. Or, you can be the first one to teach her, to pass on what you have learned from your experiences and what you believe is right and good. Then she will have a way to filter all the messages she receives."

I was twelve years old when my mom had "the sex talk" with me, which is more than what many of my friends received. While the information was biblical, accurate, and confirmed what I had heard in the third grade, it was not very relevant to me as a sixth grader. It did nothing to prepare me for the inappropriate teasing and sexual experimentation that went on during my middle school and high school years. I tried to stay out of trouble and be a "nice" girl. But time and again, I was caught off guard and ill-equipped to handle many of the situations I found myself in. I didn't feel like I had a voice. I knew the goal was to "save myself for marriage," but I did not know how to navigate the twelve-year gap between the onset of puberty and my wedding night.

It wasn't until I was in my late twenties—after an experience with a doctor who acted inappropriately and unprofessionally towards me—that I realized I had a pattern (going back to my childhood) of not knowing how to speak up. I never wanted to come across as being rude. I was more concerned about being nice than advocating for myself and possibly offending the person who was making me feel uncomfortable. Leaving the doctor's office that day, I made a decision to change this about myself. And especially because I have daughters, I decided I would do my best to equip them to speak up for themselves. I would give them a "head's up" about situations they might encounter so they could think through their responses. I would teach them to be assertive, to value safety and wisdom more than "being nice," to show respect to others and expect it in return, and to stand up for what they believe is right even when it is uncomfortable and hard. Even if it means standing alone.

We may be talking to our kids more about sex than previous generations did, but I think there is still room for improvement. Our children need us to do more than merely provide physiological facts like an encyclopedia. We need to be talking about attitudes, respect, and wisdom. As uncomfortable as these conversations may be, they need to be more prominent than the fine print on the Q-tip box that is often missed; they need to be intentional and direct. It can be tempting to wait until our kids hear about these issues and come to us with questions, but being caught off guard can be like falling into a trap. For example, if our children have never heard about pornography—what it is, the addictive nature of it, and what they need to do about it—they will not be prepared for when they are exposed to it for the first time.

So we begin with God as the designer and creator. We talk about the fall and sexual brokenness in its various forms. We teach the wisdom from Scripture that has become foolishness in the eyes of the world. And we learn to listen when our kids choose to open up rather than just talking at them. Instead of a one-time talk, these conversations become an ongoing dialogue that begins in the preschool years when our kids innocently ask, "Where do babies come from?" and continues on through their teen years. It is not always easy to know how to address some of the questions our kids throw our way, but with God's help we can do our best to converse in ways that are age-appropriate and relevant to our children's stages of development.

Healthy, God-honoring sexuality is not the only conversation we need to be having with our pre-teens and teens. If our kids have never heard about the dangers of vaping or alcohol and drug use, they will not be prepared when they are invited to try these substances for the first time. One mom I know bought a drug test and set it on the shelf in their laundry room. She told her kids, "This is a drug test, and you need to know that in this house we may do random drug tests from time to time. So if you are presented with the opportunity to use drugs, you can say, 'Oh, I can't do that. My parents do random drug testing at our house.'" In addition to setting up accountability and real-life consequences should her children choose to use drugs, she wanted to give them a way out with their peers who may be pressuring them.

Role-playing can also be helpful for kids, giving them the chance to practice how they will respond in certain situations. And walking through the "then what?" in a hypothetical scenario can help them to play it out in their heads and write their own ending ahead of time. When kids have worked through some of these possibilities in their heads and out loud, they won't be as caught off guard in an unexpected moment.

Parenting teens is not easy. These years will stretch us and challenge us like never before. We need courage to talk about the hard stuff. We need patience and perseverance to engage well even when we disagree, because we will disagree. We need the unfailing love of our heavenly Father to hold us steady when our kids try to push us away. We need his help to listen well during hard conversations and his wisdom to know the right words to speak and when to speak them. Sometimes the words our kids most need to hear are, "I love you. I'm proud of you. I'm glad you are my kid."

As our kids approach the teen years and become more independent, they may act like they don't need us. But I am convinced they need us more than ever. I don't think they want to be left to figure all this out on their own. Spending time with them over a muffin and iced tea after school or doing something active like going on a bike ride or walking the dog can create the space we need for connection. We all want to be heard, known, and loved. As we are intentional about making time for these things our relationships will be strengthened. Really listening—and *then* sincerely offering our thoughts—is a gift we can give our kids. A gift they may not ask for, but one they definitely need.

Relationship First

Life is relationships; the rest is just details.
—Gary Smalley

As our children grow and become more independent, we trade one type of chaos for another. While the early years of parenting are marked by physical exhaustion and joy as we see our little ones grow by leaps and bounds, the teen years are often marked by emotional and mental exhaustion. Our kids no longer need us to help them get dressed or brush their teeth; instead, they need to be driven around, fed ever-increasing quantities of food, and given constant reminders to get things done. They've learned basic grooming skills (though they may choose not to use them) and how to function in school and social settings, but they still need us to teach them how to drive a car, be responsible with money, and prioritize time. The cute rambling of words and adorable facial expressions we enjoyed in their younger years may be replaced with sentence fragments, one-word responses, and frequent eye rolls. Family life during the teen years brings chaos to a different level with packed schedules and everyone going in different directions. "I've got to clean up the dishes and get the kids in the bathtub" becomes "This is the third night this week we can't even sit down and have dinner together." And for families with multiple children in various stages of development, managing the daily noise and logistics during these years can make us feel like air-traffic controllers.

We have minor, recurring conflicts in our home—my grandma called it "bickering"—that we may never resolve. For example, if one child is humming or singing in the car, and another child is annoyed by it, does the happy child need to stop or does the annoyed child need to be more tolerant? Or, if someone is chewing their food in a fairly normal manner but another family member thinks the chewer is obnoxiously disgusting in the manner in which they are eating, does the chewer need to leave the table or does the annoyed party need to put on a blind fold and some noise-cancelling headphones? Understandably, opinions change depending on whether the child is the annoyed party or the one inflicting the annoying behavior. Oftentimes, after listening to the bickering, I am annoyed and order up several moments of what my mom liked to call "peace and quiet." My kids mostly hate peace and quiet.

Here is one more: If it is one child's turn to take the dog out, but the dog doesn't go to the bathroom (possibly because that child was not patient enough), does that same child need to take the dog out again two minutes later when she rings the bell? One of my daughters thinks this is how it should go, unless of course she is the one who has to go out two times in a row. Meanwhile, the dog has learned to cross her legs and wait while we keep trying to solve this conundrum.

Some conflicts, however, go deeper than minor bickering and must be resolved if the story of our family is to be healthy and whole. As a mom, often I have felt like a referee trying to mediate conflicts in our home. A striped jersey and a whistle would have come in handy for all the times I have called fouls and time-outs, reviewed footage, and tried to help our kids resolve conflicts with one another. And more than once, my emotions have gotten the best of me as I have worked to resolve my own conflicts with my daughters. Some recurring conflicts are never completely settled, but are "re" solved, again and again, as we keep working to improve communication and seek to better understand another's perspective. It may seem like we are repeating the same conflict over and over, when actually we are taking small steps forward, going deeper in our understanding and, little by little, growing in maturity.

Yet in all of the correcting, instructing, reprimanding, reminding, and discussing, in the setting of limits and following through with consequences, we must not lose sight of what is most important. Relationship is the highest priority.

During the beginning of Kate's senior year of high school, she had a set curfew and I would often wait up until she got home. A couple of nights in a row she had texted to say she was going to be late, and by the third night I was losing patience. Missing curfew seemed like it was becoming a regular occurrence, so when Kate texted me to say she and her boyfriend were in the middle of a serious conversation and she was going to be late, I said no. I asked her to come home. I told her they could finish their conversation another time. We went back and forth through text until she finally said, "I think we are breaking up. I can't leave now."

I was tired. It was the third night I had stayed up late, and I just wanted Kate to come home so I could go to bed. But I could tell from her text that she was having a hard time, and suddenly I remembered what it was like when I went through a breakup in high school. I prayed for my daughter and for the hard conversation she was having with her boyfriend, and I was moved by compassion for what Kate was going through. As more time went by, my emotions became a mix of frustration (that she still wasn't coming home) and concern for her wellbeing. When she finally texted to let me know she was on her way, I was struck with a powerful realization. *I only get one chance to do this moment well. When Kate walks through the door I can let her have it because she's an hour and a half late for the third night in a row, or I can show her that she is more important than the curfew. I can value the relationship over the rule.*

Kate walked through the door and immediately came to where I was sitting on the couch. She tucked her head under my arm, and I held her as she cried. I will never forget that moment, and I hope she won't either. We were in a hard season and had been arguing frequently. She had been pulling away from me, which is a necessary step in preparing to leave home. And I had often felt rejected, which is also a common experience for moms as they prepare to launch their kids into adulthood. For a moment, as I held my seventeen-year-old daughter, it felt like we had gone back in time to when she was a child. She still needed her mom. And I still wanted to be the one to hold her when she cried.

Rules are important. Limits are necessary. Follow-through is essential. But relationship must always take precedence over all. Preserve the relationship. Go after your teen's heart. See past the behavior to the need. Keep at it. When you get it wrong, make it right. When you fail, say you're sorry and try again. Give your teen a do-over—better yet, ask for one yourself. "Let us not become weary in doing good, for at the proper time we will reap a harvest if we do not give up" (Galatians 6:9).

Whether you are looking ahead to the teen years or are smack dab in the middle of them, author Letitia Suk encourages us to "ditch the dread." She writes, "Instead of lamenting the dire possibilities, start each day with a hope and prayer that your teen is going to be okay. Talk back to your inner critic and tell her you're doing just fine as a mom. Don't let moments of doubt turn into dreadfests. Be the yea-sayer instead of the naysayer to other moms. Expect the best and wait for it to come!" [4]

Review:

Parenting teens is challenging, but so are other stages of parenthood. So we keep learning and growing. We continue to rely on our friends, learning from those who are further along on this journey, as well as those who are in the same season as us and facing similar challenges. We ask God for wisdom. And when we feel like we are in over our heads, we reach out and ask for help. We have made it through the hard stuff of other seasons, and *we will make it through these years.*

Reflect:

1. Which stage of parenting has been the most enjoyable for you so far? Which has been the most challenging?

2. Are there issues you avoid talking about with your kids, and if so, how can you engage well and give direct communication a prominent place in your relationships?

3. How do you balance the need for rules, limits, and consequences while preserving the relationship and pursuing connection with your child?

Respond:

God, thank you for your faithfulness in every season of parenting. Help me not to dread what is to come, but to trust that you will equip me and help me every step of this journey. Give me wisdom in every situation, provide resources for every need, and bless my relationships with my children. May your grace work its way into every conversation and every heart. Amen.

#6—Stay Balanced

The Illusion of Balance

Being a mother, as far as I can tell, is a constantly
evolving process of adapting to the needs of your child
while also changing and growing as a person
in your own right.
—Deborah Insel

We talk about "finding balance" as if it is something that is actually attainable, as if once we find it we can stop looking for it. As moms, we may imagine that finding our balance is like riding a bicycle—we just need to steer the handlebars and stay upright while we pedal. Of course, we mustn't forget to look out for all the other bikers weaving in and out of our lane while simultaneously avoiding potholes and debris in the road. Did I mention the crying infant strapped in the baby Bjorn, and the older child buckled in the bike trailer, yelling that he needs to go to the bathroom, and our arms full of everyone else's stuff? After all, children do view mothers as garbage receptacles.

As amusing as this image is, I wonder if surfing might be a better analogy than riding a bike? To be clear, I have never gone surfing, but I think the visual works nicely because just when we think we have our babies on a sleep schedule or our preteens figured out, they start to cut a tooth or puberty comes knocking on their door. Just when we think we've got the consistent family dinner thing down, softball season begins and nutritious, organized meals go out the window. Just when we think we've nailed the college launch process, our second child leaves for college and we are thrown into a pre-empty nest sort of crisis we weren't expecting. Just when we think we've finally found some level of balance in our lives, a wave we didn't see knocks us off our surfboard. Our kids get sick. Anxiety or depression sets in. Our car—or marriage—breaks down. Journaling, yoga, soothing music, hot baths, and diffusers filling every room in our house with the scent of lavender can help to temporarily decrease our stress levels, but the sense of inner calm and balance we are looking for can feel perpetually out of reach.

We can do our best to create some degree of order and calm in our lives and in our homes, but the reality is that, even with our best efforts, chaos will find us. Some hectic seasons are unavoidable. When our daughter is playing softball, it feels like our whole life revolves around softball, with practices and games almost every day. When a member of the family is struggling, it often requires a disproportionate amount of our time and energy as we come alongside and offer help and support. Sometimes work projects or home renovations consume us for a season, and any semblance of "normal life" goes out the window. Even in the process of writing this book, there were weeks on end when my life felt out of balance. Late nights of writing left me groggy the following mornings, and I spent too many daytime hours to count, hunkered down at the kitchen table with my laptop. I missed out on time with family and friends. I didn't clean the house for days. I let things pile up. We had "whatever" for dinner several evenings a week. And though it was necessary to meet my deadlines and finish writing this book, I knew that it was a temporary period of time. I couldn't support that kind of intense focus on my work while neglecting everything (and everyone) else in my life.

So how do we approach this craving we have for balance and order, in light of the reality that our kids, our schedules, and life around us are constantly evolving? Because even in our diligence to create structure and order, life will happen. The first lessons our children teach us when we become mothers is that we are not in control, and we need to become flexible and adaptable. Perfect balance is unattainable, so let's start with what we *can* control. We can intentionally make choices every day that align with our values. We can look at—and work to accept—our own limitations and our unique wirings, as well as those of our husbands and children. We can create margin in our lives for the unexpected and make wise choices about how we live out our days. Our calendars are a really good place to start.

Most of us have seen television programs where a professional organizer is called in to help a family that has been overcome by clutter. Stuff has overtaken the space in these people's homes, and the ensuing chaos is more than just material. It's not only that they cannot find their keys or remote control or that rodents are living behind boxes and under piles of clothes: their overload is causing *overwhelm*. When you hear their stories, you can see the ripple effect of how the clutter and hoarding are negatively impacting their health and their relationships. We understand the idea of spatial limitations. We can't fill up every square inch of our homes and our garages with stuff and expect to experience tranquility.

Similarly, we understand the financial concept of living within our means. We know that spending more than we make is foolish and will result in financial hardship. We see the wisdom in putting money aside for unanticipated expenses. While we recognize the importance of creating margin in these areas of our lives, when it comes to our calendars, however, we forget that we also have a limited amount of time and energy. We forget that our kids have limited capacities as well. Many of us are flying through life at a pace that is simply not sustainable—not for us as parents, and not for our kids. Our days are over-booked, our calendars are filled with activities and appointments, and for many of us, our overloaded schedules are causing us to feel overwhelmed. We fall into bed each night, exhausted from our long days, but we find it difficult to really rest. More than a third of American adults are not getting enough sleep on a regular basis,[5] and more than 40 million American adults are suffering from anxiety.[6]

Limits are everywhere. They are a part of life, and trying to resist or ignore them results in real—and sometimes serious—consequences. For example, we are required to abide by speed limits and blood alcohol limits when driving: if we ignore these, we may face legal repercussions. Airlines enforce weight limits for checked bags, and exceeding those limits will cost us. When we overstuff our bags (sometimes even sitting on them to close them), zippers break, and stuff spills out. In a similar way, when we overstuff our lives with too much stress and activity, stuff spills out: anger, impatience, irritability, fatigue, addictions, anxiety, and depression. Our physical, mental, and relational health suffer when we do not live within our means. We must intentionally create space in our calendars for rest, recreation, life-giving connection with God and others, spiritual practices, and down-time. We need it, and our kids need it.

Kids can be a good gauge for assessing whether or not our schedules are too crammed with activities and commitments. When our children complain about being tired, don't want to go to extra-curricular activities, or express feeling anxious about homework or school, it would be wise for us to slow down and evaluate whether our calendars are too full. When I talk about this topic with other moms, I hear stories of kids refusing to go to Karate class and begging to stay home and have a game or movie night. While it's true that members of the same family will most likely have differing energy levels, drives, and temperaments, I think it is also true that each of us, including our children, has a God-given sensor that warns us when we are living life near or at capacity. Some of us are dangerously close to exceeding our limits.

When my youngest daughter, Brenna, started first grade, I began working part-time outside our home. With fewer hours at home during the week, I often fell behind on daily chores and errands. In order to keep up, my afternoons and evenings were often peppered with tasks like grocery shopping, household cleaning, and laundry. Brenna noticed my attention was divided and started to write herself into my day planner. I'd flip the calendar page to next week and see Brenna's handwriting in big letters nearly filling up Tuesday's box, "Spend time with Brenna." It was really cute, but I could feel a heavy dose of mom guilt settling over me.

I took some time to process the guilt, holding on to what was helpful, and letting go of condemnation. I realized I didn't need to crumble in a ball and cry my eyes out because I was a bad mom. I didn't need to quit my job or hire a cleaning service. I was adjusting to starting a new job, and it was *good* for the family to step up and pitch in. It was good for me to step out, do something I enjoyed with other adults, and contribute to our household income. But, in addition to all that understanding, grace, and telling myself the truth, I also sensed a warning. *Pay attention here. Your daughter misses you. Take some time just for her on Tuesday, and write her in the calendar the following week.* Sometimes our children have a better sense than we do of their needs and limits, and it's important to listen to their verbal and non-verbal cues. If they never complain about being bored, we may be too busy.

We can become so accustomed to the frantic pull of our culture to be busy, to be in a hurry, and to move from one activity to the next, that we don't even realize there is another way to live. Our family lives in a suburb outside of Chicago. The schools are excellent, and though we love the community where we live, from the time the girls were very young we began to notice the competitive culture in which we were raising them. It wasn't enough to sign up your four-year-old for preschool. Most kids were in multiple activities like dance and gymnastics, soccer and T-ball. Language programs were offered as part of an extension program after school so our kids could learn Spanish or Mandarin.

At first, we saw no harm in having our children try different activities or move into advanced classes in school. It seemed healthy to keep them busy, allow them to figure out what they liked, and push them to excel. After a while, though, we began to hear inklings from other parents that if we wanted our kids to get into good colleges, they needed to be on the advanced track in middle school and take every high honors and AP class offered them in high school. If we wanted them to play sports as teens, we needed to get them into every camp and clinic available from the earliest age possible. It wasn't enough to sign them up for park district programs; they needed to play on travel teams. They needed to join a professional academy or company to develop their talent if we wanted them to succeed.

I started to see the stress this mentality can put on kids and parents alike. Not everyone thrives under pressure: some people crumble. I began to hear other parents complain about the rat race, as well as the amount of money required to fund all these activities. Every weeknight was spent practicing some sport, going to some club, and completing hours of homework. Every weekend was spent traveling to out-of-town games and tournaments. Things like family dinner and Saturday morning pancakes and church on Sunday were just not possible with such a rigorous schedule.

Over the years, our family has sometimes stuck out like a sore thumb as we have strived to live within our limited resources of time, energy, and finances. Though Bernie's multiple sclerosis has been in remission for many years, the first several years after his diagnosis were laden with relapses, hospitalizations, and the trial and error process of finding the right therapeutic medications and doses. Living with chronic illness, in some ways, has forced us to take our foot off the gas. It has required us to budget our time, money, and energy more carefully. Sometimes this has meant that our children didn't get the name brand clothing their friends got, because we couldn't afford it. Sometimes, it meant saying no to having sleepovers, because Bernie needed to rest. Other times, it meant not being able to join a travel sports team or private dance company, because the time and financial commitment were too high. When the girls were younger, they each tried various activities in order to discover their interests and talents, but the general rule in our family has been one activity per child, per season.

At times, I have felt guilty that we did not give our kids some of the same opportunities many of their friends were receiving. As they got older, they were not always prepared to compete with peers who had been vigorously training for many years. But the choices we've made over the years, though not always easy, have reflected our priorities and values. We value faith and family. We believe in living within our means. Taking care of our physical and mental health is a priority. Date nights and family dinner get written on the calendar. Consistent attendance and involvement in our home church has helped us build a faith foundation and relationships that have endured.

There is not one right formula for how many activities parents should allow their children to participate in, or how many nights per week a family gathers around the table to share a meal. Each family is unique, and each season brings specific challenges and demands. Some seasons, such as caring for aging parents, grieving the loss of a loved one, seeking treatment for a physical or mental health challenge, moving to a new home, or welcoming a new child require more from us. During these times we often need to scale back, to say no to certain things so we will have the time, energy, and resources to fully step into our current reality with all its joys and challenges.

Finding balance is less about achieving some mystical level of calm and more about making choices every day that align with our values and our goals. It's about regularly assessing where we are at with our stress and energy levels, and then prayerfully discerning when to say yes and when to say no. It's about recognizing when we are veering off track and then making adjustments to course correct. What do we want our families to look like five and ten years down the road? These dreams begin today. The squares on our calendars are like bricks on a path leading to our future.

This means that on a Tuesday when I feel overwhelmed by the rest of the week laid out before me, I stop and take inventory. I consider the challenging day I had on Monday and the fact that I didn't sleep well Monday night. I evaluate my stress level. I pay attention to my body and my emotions and my thoughts. I tune in to the whispers of the Holy Spirit who says, "Slow down. Be careful here. Take some time to be still. Start your day with prayer. Eat a good lunch. Take some time to connect with a friend this week. Read your Bible. Go for a walk. Go on a date with your husband. Go to bed early tonight."

As moms, life will continue to be crazy, busy, challenging, and stressful. We will never get it all together or feel like we are finally on top of it all. No matter how hard we try, we will not find perfect balance. Even if we think we've momentarily found it, we certainly won't be able to maintain it. But we can make adjustments. Like the surfer, we perceive the flow of the constantly changing water and try our best to ride the unpredictable waves. We follow the unique course God is leading us on, which will look different at times than the course of the surfer next to us. When we are knocked under and fall off our boards, we get back on and catch the next one, knowing the Maker of the seas is stronger than the waves.

The seas have lifted up, Lord,
    the seas have lifted up their voice;
the seas have lifted up their pounding waves.

Mightier than the thunder of the great waters,
    mightier than the breakers of the sea
the Lord on high is mighty.

                    (Psalm 93:3-4)

Tiny Houses and Quiet Spaces

Living loved is sourced in your quiet daily surrender to the One who made you.
—Lysa TerKeurst

When I watch *Tiny House Hunters,* I fantasize about what it would be like to own one. I love the idea of simplifying, minimizing our footprint on this earth, getting rid of excess stuff, and living below our means. I would, however, have some concerns about the practicality of our family living in a house that is less than two hundred and fifty square feet and uses a composting toilet. I think that, like a new prescription drug, we'll have to wait awhile to fully understand the long-term risks and side effects associated with moving your entire family (pets included) into a house the size of a shed.

I know that realistically, for our family, the immediate effects of living in a tiny house would be disastrous (mostly because of me). I'm an introvert, and the truth is, if we ever did get a tiny house, I'd want to live in it alone. Not every day, of course—I love my family—but maybe once a week. Or an occasional three-day weekend.

That I can admit my need for solitude is a sign of personal growth, because for a long time I have felt guilt over needing time and space to myself. I have often felt like something must be wrong with me because I do not enjoy ladies' night out with the other moms from school; I would much rather meet one or two friends for coffee. For years I've avoided going to our annual block party, but I love when I run into one of the neighbors when walking the dog and we stand on the sidewalk for twenty minutes and chat. When I feel really depleted, sometimes I want to stay home on Sunday morning (and have the house all to myself) because we go to a megachurch with thousands of other people, and crowds exhaust me.

One year, over Christmas break, after having had a group of teenagers and young adults in our home several days in a row, I felt terrible telling my daughters that the kids needed to find another house to go to that night. I love my kids' friends, and I always wanted our house to be the one where they all want to hang out. But with the stress of the holidays, several overnight guests, various social events, and all the noise and commotion that accompany these things, I had a headache that wouldn't let up for two days straight. And as I stared out our kitchen window while washing the dishes, I wondered if we could renovate our kids' playhouse into a tiny house. A farm-house style retreat just for me to get away once in a while.

Solitude is good for my soul, but sometimes I resent my need for it. I wish I could be more outgoing, more of a "people person." I wish I could be more comfortable in social situations. But being an introvert doesn't mean I hate people. It doesn't mean I'm shy. It doesn't mean that I don't value and need connection with others. It means that I tend to be energized by spending time alone (or with someone one-on-one), and that being with people tends to be draining for me.

The thing is, even though I wrestle with these self-critical thoughts, I believe God *made* me an introvert. I believe it is part of the way he uniquely designed me. And while it's important to grow and at times push myself out of my comfort zone, my wiring is not faulty or something that needs to be fixed. It needs to be *nurtured*. I don't need to apologize for my personality or the way I am. Quite the opposite, I need to better understand my God-given design and practice voicing my needs. As I accept and appreciate the way God made me, I can better care for myself in ways that fill me up.

Because when nurtured and cared for, this wiring also makes me introspective and insightful, caring and a good listener. This wiring is one of the reasons I am a writer.

In our family, we are learning to value our differences. and that begins with understanding ourselves and each other. We enjoy taking personality tests and talking about the enneagram. Our daughters are especially fascinated by the way these assessments make sense of how we are wired (though we still can't quite pin my husband down), and they help us understand one other better. It makes sense that one of my daughters is crabby because she's been around people non-stop while the other one is down in the dumps because she hasn't seen her friends in several days. I understand why Bernie makes new friends every time he goes to Starbucks while I avoid eye contact with anyone I don't know. When we understand one another better, we judge one another less.

For busy moms, solitude is hard to come by. When my daughters were preschoolers, I would structure a little time for myself during naps or quiet time in the afternoons (my kids mostly resisted quiet time). Later, when the girls went to school, I found pockets of time here and there, but as activities picked up and I began working a few days a week out of our home, time to myself became a rarity. And in recent years, as we are nearing the empty-nest season, Bernie and I both work from home a couple of days a week, on the same days. We have an open concept living space and my husband has to make frequent conference and phone calls while I am trying to write, so . . . you get the picture. We do a fair amount of negotiating and taking turns moving around the house. On the rare occasion that I find myself home alone, it's exhilarating. It's energizing. I love the peace and quiet. I love to write and not be interrupted. I love to read. I even enjoy tasks like cooking and cleaning in total silence. Time alone replenishes my soul.

I'm getting better at figuring out what I need and then voicing those needs—not in a demanding way, insisting that other people meet them, but in a curious, accepting way. Right before I sat down to write this chapter, Bernie called. He had picked up our daughter and her friend for lunch, dropped them back at school, and was calling to ask me a kind and beautiful question. He had a proposition that made my heart soar.

"Would you like to have some time alone?"

"I wouldn't mind," I replied. "Why, what are you doing?"

"Well, if you'd like to have the house to yourself, I could go to the coffee shop and do some work before I pick up the girls from school."

"That would be great," I told him. And then I ate my leftover beef burgundy while watching *House Hunters*, cleaned the floors, and then hunkered down in the kitchen and wrote in silence until the family came home. It was heaven.

I don't know what marriage experts would think of this, but I think it's extraordinary. It's wonderful to be understood. It's amazing to be valued and loved just the way I am. Maybe even *because* of the way I am. A little understanding goes a long way. Perhaps I don't need to build a "she shed" after all. Small, regular doses of quiet space, found early in the morning before the house comes alive, captured late at night after everyone has gone to bed, or given as a gift on an ordinary day from my understanding, extroverted husband, may be just enough to satisfy my tiny house dreams.

The Problem with Self-Care

I am the vine; you are the branches. If you remain in me
and I in you, you will bear much fruit; apart from me
you can do nothing.
—John 15:5

I survived my first week with two daughters away at college. We had done college drop-offs before with our eldest (and they were *hard*), but after a really great summer with everyone at home, transitioning from a household of five to a household of three hit me harder than I could have prepared for. And it didn't help that our youngest, a freshman in high school and a social butterfly, was hardly ever home. Quiet dinners for two, with just my husband and me sitting across from each other at the table, accentuated my feelings of loss. Our family was changing and would never be the same.

Those close to me had lovingly advised that I practice good self-care. They had encouraged me to do things that fill my bucket and to be kind to myself, because it was going to be a hard week. I took their advice to heart and had every intention of laying low, taking it easy, and giving myself the space and time to process my feelings about my baby birds leaving the nest. It turned out to be a hard week, indeed, but not only for the reasons I expected.

A family we know suffered an unimaginable loss that rocked us to our core. Someone I love was hurting and needed my time. I sensed God nudging me to visit a friend who had cancer. I hadn't seen her in weeks because I was busy getting my girls ready to fly the coop and doing the things we do during summer. It was a hard week filled with the kinds of things that tend to be emotionally draining, but at the end of the week, to my surprise, my bucket didn't feel empty. My soul actually felt nourished. God lovingly provided the energy, strength, friendship, and prayer I needed to move through each day, taking one thing at a time, doing the things he was calling me to do. Two mornings in a row, friends called to pray with me just when I needed it. I felt connected not only to these dear women, but to our life-giving God who provides, protects, and gives us everything we need so that we can do what he has called us to do.

Self-care, from a human perspective, is all about assessing our human limitations and needs for sleep, rest, good food, exercise, relational connection, solitude, recreation, etc. . . . and then being intentional to meet those needs. It's about self-awareness. And though all of these things are really good and healthy, focusing on these things alone will not fill our buckets or our souls.

We are called to love God with all our heart, soul, mind, and strength, and to love others as we love ourselves (Luke 10:27). These are not small endeavors. If I really want to love God and love others as myself—if I want these to be the pursuits of my heart, and love to be the driving force in my life—then my daily schedules and to-do lists must include time and space for my relationships with God and others, as well as healthy self-care (loving others *as myself*). But what does healthy self-care even look like? Is it really as simple as the airplane analogy of putting the oxygen mask on myself first, before I help others? Is it pampering myself at a spa every couple of months or treating myself to that expensive bag I've had my eye on, because I'm worth it? And how exactly does this fit with Jesus' call for me to deny myself, take up my cross, and follow him (Luke 9:23)? How does putting myself first line up with Jesus' words to lose my life for him that I may find it (Luke 9:24)? These are hard teachings, and for exhausted moms who feel like we are constantly pouring ourselves out on behalf of our children and those around us, this seems impossible to pull off.

It is a widely-held belief that we can't love others until we first love ourselves. But that is only a partial truth. There is an order to what Jesus is saying that we need to pay attention to. The first and greatest commandment is to love God with all that we are. Yet, John reminds us that we can only truly love because he first loved us (1 John 4:19). Our love for God, for others, and even for ourselves flows out of having been loved first by him. It is only when we receive his love for us that we can then love him in response, and love others as we have been loved. Those who are deeply loved are free to deeply love. This distinction may seem small, but it is profound. We do not begin with self-love. We begin with God's love for us and then remain in it, abide in it, and live daily in it (John 15).

Jesus experienced human limitations and needs just like us. He needed sleep and rest and food. He needed friendship and solitude just like we do. He needed time alone in prayer. And yet, because his purpose was always to do the will of his Father, his days and moments were directed by the Spirit. Time and again we see his attempts to take care of his human needs interrupted by people's needs and God's higher purposes. (As a mom, you are undoubtedly experiencing these interruptions several times a day!)

Before beginning his ministry, Jesus retreated to the wilderness where he was tempted by the devil. He performed his first miraculous sign while attending a wedding as a *guest*. After he began his ministry, he pulled away for times of solitude and then was immediately bombarded by crowds of people with needs. On one occasion, he fell asleep from exhaustion on a boat, then was woken up by his panic-stricken disciples because of a violent storm. Another time, he stopped to rest at a well: tired, thirsty, and hungry, he struck up a conversation with a woman while his disciples went to get food. His self-care was always within the context of his higher purpose and calling—to do the will of his Father. The eating and the sleeping and the solitude—they were all subject to his obedience to his Father in each moment. Which meant that while he was preparing to enter into his season of ministry, he faced spiritual opposition. While he was waiting for lunch, he asked a woman for a drink of water and then, recognizing her spiritual thirst, engaged in a conversation that transformed her life, and later, her whole village. And while trying to get some much-needed sleep on a boat, and immediately after being woken by his disciples, he silenced a raging storm, demonstrating that "even the wind and the waves obey him" (Luke 8:25).

Jesus went to great lengths and used powerful imagery to explain to his followers his dependency on his Father.

So Jesus explained, "I tell you the truth, the Son can do nothing by himself. He does only what he sees the Father doing. Whatever the Father does, the Son also does." (John 5:19)

"I don't speak on my own authority. The Father who sent me has commanded me what to say and how to say it." (John 12:49)

So Jesus said, "When you have lifted up the Son of Man on the cross, then you will understand that I Am he. I do nothing on my own but say only what the Father taught me." (John 8:28)

In John 15, Jesus uses the imagery of a vine and branches to show our need to remain in him, to be connected to the true source of life. How foolish it would be to cut a branch off of a vine, lay it on a table, and then spray it with water, sprinkle plant food over it, and shine a spotlight on it, hoping it will grow. And yet, if we go through our days disconnected from the true Vine, even our best attempts at self-care will be fruitless. Jesus is the source of life, and apart from him we can do nothing. When we live from a place of abiding in him and staying connected to him, he provides everything we need to do his will. He gives strength and energy even when we are tired and weary. When we remain in him and in his love, we can find purpose even in the interruptions.

It is essential that we take care of ourselves. It is good to have self-awareness. It is important to understand the unique ways in which we are wired and be intentional about our choices. Nevertheless, solely focusing on meeting our needs will not fill our buckets or protect us from depletion. When we love and serve others out of the abundance of first having been loved by God, when we are connected to him as we expend energy and give of our time, he fills us. He satisfies our deepest longings and provides for all our needs. He replenishes our depleted resources and restores our souls. He reorients our priorities and guides our everyday decision-making. He overflows our buckets with living water that won't ever run dry.

The challenge is to discern where God is leading, obediently follow, and then commit to doing our best in each of those areas. When we lay our heads on our pillows at the end of each day, whether we changed diapers, taught a classroom full of kids, met a friend for coffee, played make-believe with our preschooler, or put in a full day at the office, may we have the satisfaction of knowing we spent our days doing what God asked us to do. Then we can rest, knowing we have lived creatively, loved whole-heartedly, and followed Him unswervingly. And on those days when we come up short, miss the mark, or fall off our boards, we can still rest. Because tomorrow is a new day, and we are dearly loved.

> Because of the LORD's great love we are not consumed,
>   for his compassions never fail.
> They are new every morning;
>   great is your faithfulness.

(Lamentations 3:22-23)

Review:

Perfect balance is unattainable, so let's start with what we *can* control. We can intentionally make choices every day that align with our values. We can look at—and work to accept—our own limitations and our unique wirings, as well as those of our husbands and children. We can create margin in our lives for the unexpected and make wise choices about how we live out our days.

Reflect:

1. When you consider your family's unique circumstances, combination of personalities, and limitations of time, finances, and energy, how do these factors expand your idea of "living within your means?"

2. What spills out of you when you overstuff your life and do not pay attention to your limits? Where might overload be causing overwhelm?

3. How does the imagery of the vine and the branches shape your view of self-care? What does "filling your bucket" look like in light of what it means to be connected to the true source of life and love (Jesus), looking to him to satisfy, restore, and fill you with living water that won't ever run dry?

Respond:

God, thank you that in the midst of constantly changing seasons you remain the same. Your love is steadfast, and you are my ever-present help. Help me to make choices each day that align with our family's values and your will for our lives. Help me to abide in you and remain in your love, that I may experience your peace even in the midst of chaos. Amen.

#7—Kids Come First—You Can Work on Your Marriage Later

One Inch Scale

By wisdom a house is built,
and through understanding it is established;
through knowledge its rooms are filled
with rare and beautiful treasures.
—Proverbs 24:3-4

Several years ago, a friend of mine dropped off a few items she wanted to sell at my garage sale, including an old dollhouse that came with a Ziploc bag of miscellaneous pieces and mostly broken furniture. She asked if I wanted it, and though I entertained the idea, I figured my girls probably would not play with it. Besides, I was trying to *unload* our extra belongings, not acquire new things. We slapped a steal-of-a-deal price on it, and I knew someone would snatch it right up. That someone turned out to be my sister, Kari, who lives in northern Michigan. She called to ask how the garage sale was going, and when I told her about the dollhouse, she was ecstatic. She wanted it. Would I keep it for her in my basement for a month or two until she came to Chicago to visit? Of course I would. Sold—to my sister for $15.

That dollhouse, in need of some creative loving care, sat in my basement for several weeks. Every time I went down to use my treadmill, I thought about how much Kari was going to love it. I'd stop and look at the tiny little pieces. A lot of the furniture was broken, but there were also several cute little kitchen items: a speckled sky-blue coffee pot with tiny matching coffee cups, hand-painted pitchers and platters, and copper buckets. A little red oil lamp, pots and pans, and brooms made out of toothpicks and straw. The more I went downstairs and looked at this little house, the more I started wishing I had snatched it up myself.

After a lovely visit with Kari and her family a couple of months later, she loaded the dollhouse in the back of their SUV and drove away. I didn't think about it again until one day when I was walking through Hobby Lobby and I saw *them*. In the back, left corner of the store, displayed high above all the other merchandise, was a breathtaking collection of fully assembled, beautifully decorated dollhouses that left my sister's dollhouse in the dust.

For my 38th birthday, I asked my husband and kids for a dollhouse kit from Hobby Lobby. I chose the Vermont Farmhouse, a modest selection, not the fanciest Victorian model, but not the one that looked like a gingerbread house either. It was somewhere in the middle, kind of like my real house, except this one had what I have always wanted—a porch. I left it in the box for a month or two, because as much as I wanted to start working on it, it intimidated me.

For my first step, I took all the pieces out of the box, labeled everything, and read the instructions cover to cover. Then I let the pieces sit there for several more days while I mustered up the courage to start painting, wallpapering, and finally, gluing. The gluing was the scariest part of the whole process, because it was so permanent. If the walls went up even slightly crooked, the entire building would be off, and it would look more like a haunted house than a lovely dollhouse.

I used leftover paint from our real house, and my daughters designed and helped paint the three rooms in the attic—one for each of them. I stained the hardwood floors, wallpapered the kitchen, and painted the front door red. I chose light gray with white trim for the exterior of the house. I dyed the shingles gray and enlisted Bernie's help with gluing them on. Together, using a hot glue gun for the first time, we successfully shingled the roof. The kit was expertly built, with precise cuts and measurements, everything going together without a hitch. It gave Bernie and me a false sense of confidence, like maybe we should start volunteering with Habitat for Humanity now that we'd shingled a roof and built a porch.

My friend, the previous owner of the dollhouse that started this new-found obsession, thought I was a little off my rocker. She called me one night when I was wallpapering the kitchen, and when I told her what I was doing, said, "Oh, how nice . . . how 'bout you come over to my real house and help me take *down* the wallpaper in my *real* kitchen?"

I couldn't explain why, but it was so satisfying and fun to build this house with my own hands, to choose the layout and size of each room, where the stairs would go, and which colors would go where. My daughters loved it, too. They each contributed in different ways, mixing colors, painting, and setting up furniture. We put white rocking chairs on the porch flanking a small table and set a pitcher of lemonade on it with a couple of glasses. We bought miniature clay flowerpots and tiny scraps of fake flowers. I made an area rug out of leftover fabric from our piano bench. I fashioned a wreath out of a strip of berry garland. My proudest moment, when I realized the full scope of my creativity, was when I made a toilet paper holder using a toothpick and sculpting clay, and mini-toilet paper rolls using real toilet paper. I began looking around my big house for items I could replicate to a one-inch scale and use as furnishings in my little house, all the while thinking, *Who does this? I must be crazy.* . . .

At the risk of sounding strange, I think my love for this dollhouse runs soul deep. Having worked on it for hours, I could almost imagine what it would be like to be miniature myself: sitting on the porch sipping lemonade, walking through the red front door into the living room, then going left into the kitchen. I'd fill up my copper tea kettle with water from my farmhouse sink and sweep my hardwood floors with my straw broom while the water boiled. I'd make my way up the stairs, through the master bedroom with the brass bed and the lovely wreath above the armoire, into the bathroom. Then, I'd drink my tea while bathing in the claw-foot tub, right in front of the window. (I'm miniature, so no one would be able to see me.)

For me, this feeling of *home* is all about family and my deep longing for connection. It's the same longing I've had at times walking through my neighborhood. I see a driveway with several cars in it on a Saturday morning, and I imagine a family gathered around a kitchen table for a weekend breakfast—high school football players with enormous appetites and younger siblings with sticky fingers. I can almost hear their conversation, everyone sharing about their week or their plans for the day: yard work, soccer games, or a barbeque later that afternoon. I know this may not be reality—the people in those houses may be zoned out in front of the TV, totally disconnected from one another or at each other's throats. The family I grew up in officially fell apart when I was in college. I love my family, and I have accepted the present reality, but I still carry some sadness. I still yearn for family as God intended, unbroken and whole.

In some ways, building a family is a lot like building that dollhouse. We have a vision and a dream of what we want to create, and we get to make choices along the way that determine just what our "relational houses" will look like.

Most of us start off married life focused on our relationship as husband and wife, and then when our kids come along, our priorities inevitably shift. More than anything, we want to create a family where our children can thrive in every way. We want to meet all their needs and give them every opportunity to explore, learn, and grow. We want to give them the world, in the hopes that someday, when they leave our home and go out into the world, they will be equipped to do what God has created them to do—to be the people God made them to be. These are the years of exhaustion and exhilaration, when most of our time and attention is focused on our children. Yet, in the daily grind of parenting, we often allow our marriages to be pushed to the back burner. *We need to focus on our kids right now. We're just so busy! And tired. Who has time to work on their marriage, anyway? Someday we'll have time for each other. Someday things will be better.* But the truth is, if we don't pay attention to our marriage during these years, we may not have much of a marriage left by the time our kids leave us.

One of the very best things we can do for our children is to invest in our marriages. The specific things we do will vary from couple to couple, and different seasons of marriage will require unique attention. For some, it might mean working through relational issues and past hurts, which may include seeking individual and/or couple's counseling. We may need to learn how to improve the way we communicate and resolve conflict. When dealing with loss, addictions, serious illnesses, and specific challenges, we might want to join a support group to walk with others who are going through something similar. For all of us, it means being intentional to make time together a priority. Regularly scheduled dates can give us the time we need to connect, have fun, dream together, and remember why we fell in love in the first place. It doesn't have to be a formal event in the evening—it could be breakfast, lunch, or a coffee date during the week.

Parents with young children may find it difficult to carve out time to spend together as a couple, especially if childcare is not easily available. Bernie and I have never lived close to our extended families, so when our kids were little, we started a babysitting co-op with three other families. Friday nights were date nights—one couple would watch all the kids at their house while the other couples went out on individual dates. It was a win-win for both parents and kids; the kids got to play with their friends, and the parents got three dates a month without having to pay for childcare.

Nurturing the friendships we started with our spouses before we got married and had children is essential if we want to build our homes with wisdom and understanding. Learning how to love each other better is one of the ways we fill the rooms with rare and beautiful treasures. This takes time, consistency, and patience.

I have a sign in my real house that says, "Home is where your story begins," and it reminds me that marriage and parenting are not all about me. The choices I make today will impact my family in the future. This is sobering because so often I don't get it right. My kids are broken in some ways because I am broken. My husband is broken. We long to be whole and complete, but we are still a work in progress.

Even still, that family I dream of—I'm living in it. Those are *our* kids gathered around the breakfast table on a Saturday morning, eating pancakes with maple butter and bacon, and talking about their plans for the weekend. Those are *our* kids looking across the table at us—at two imperfect people who became husband and wife before they became parents and were pronounced Mr. and Mrs. before they were ever called Daddy and Mommy. Our children are counting on us to build something together that will last a lifetime, one Saturday morning breakfast at a time.

Christians are not Immune

"In this world you will have trouble. . . ."
—Jesus, John 16:33

"What is the best thing parents can do for their kids?" This is the question one of my college professors asked on the first day of class. I went to a Christian college, and several students immediately responded with some version of the answer, "Raise them up in the ways of the Lord." Obviously, that was a great answer. Ultimately, the best thing any of us can do in this life is point people to Jesus. However, this is an opinion question with not just one right answer, and the way we answer questions like this reveals our passions, our convictions, and often times, our wounds. Sitting in class that day, I had another answer immediately come to mind.

I was nineteen years old, thousands of miles away from home, and I had just found out that my parents were getting divorced. I was devastated. I knew our family would never be the same. I knew that the next time I went home, it would be different. I knew it would *forever* be different. As I sat in class that day, listening to the other students discussing their opinions and then listening to the professor unpack his answer, every word he spoke resonated with what I was thinking, how I was feeling, and what I believed. "The best thing parents can do for their children is to love each other well. Because if parents can do that, their children will be far more likely to adopt their values as their own. They will be more inclined to follow the footsteps of faith their parents walked before them. And they will be more equipped to create loving, healthy relationships in their own lives if loving, healthy relationships were modeled for them at home."

The news of my parents' divorce broke my heart, but it did not come as a surprise. For as long as I could remember, I had been afraid that my parents would split up. I was about five years old when I looked up at my mother, who was standing in front of the dryer folding clothes, and asked, "Mommy, are you and Daddy going to get divorced?" My question startled her. She stopped folding the laundry, bent down, and pulled me into a hug. "Oh, honey, . . . no, Daddy and I are not getting divorced. Why would you ask me that?"

I asked the question because I knew, even at that young age, that my parents' marriage was rocky, and our family was in trouble. We went to church several times a week. We prayed before meals and at bedtime. We hosted Bible studies in our home and my parents had a deep faith in Christ. But few knew what was really going on in private, between Sundays and behind closed doors. There was chaos, fighting, and out-of-control anger. As a little girl, I saw and heard traumatic things that little girls don't know what to do with. More than once, I'd woken from a sound sleep late at night to the sounds of fighting, my heart pounding, everything in me rising to high-alert—*Will this be the night our family falls apart?*

There was a gap between what we believed in our family and what was being lived out in our home. As a child, I struggled to make sense of this incongruity, and as I observed other families, my thinking became very black and white. I would pay attention to married couples at church and observe my friends' parents, and I subconsciously placed every family I knew in one of two categories: nearly-perfect or messed up like mine. There was no in-between.

My parents separated for a year when I was in high school, then got back together for a couple of years before divorcing when I was in college. At my twenty-year high school reunion, several former classmates told me how shocked they were when my parents got divorced. "You guys were so religious. You seemed like the perfect family." I realized then that I was not the only one who had made up stories about other people's families. It's so easy to assume other people have it all together.

I met Bernie when I was in college, and a few years later, I went into my own marriage hoping we could create the family I had always longed for. Bernie and I read books on how to have successful relationships. We joined a marriage group at church. We were committed to building a marriage that would last a lifetime.

Our first few years of marriage were smooth sailing; then life got really hard, really fast. During a four-year period, we experienced the pain of miscarriage, the uncertainty that comes with job loss, the stress that accompanies a cross-country move, and the helplessness that arises when a spouse battles anxiety and depression. We celebrated with great joy the births of our first two daughters in the midst of these changes and losses, and then came the blow that nearly took us out—Bernie was diagnosed with multiple sclerosis. These stressors and major life events brought out wounds, fears, and behaviors we didn't know we had in us. As our family began to "settle," I began to see some cracks. I noticed some gaps between the *ideal* of who we wanted to be and the *reality* of what we lived out daily in our home.

We wanted to handle conflict in healthy, respectful ways; instead, we repeated unhealthy, destructive patterns we carried with us from our original families into our marriage. We wanted to forgive each other and let go of past offenses; instead, the offenses accumulated causing resentment on both sides. We were unprepared to navigate the life challenges that came our way, as well as our personality and cultural differences. We were ill-equipped to recover from the hurt we were causing one another. We desired to be self-controlled, but far too often our emotions got the best of us. We wanted to be loving and selfless, but time and again we protected and defended ourselves at all costs. *How could marriage between two Christians be so difficult?*

Bernie and I became stuck in a destructive "dance" of unresolved conflict and hurt. The pattern of our back and forth steps was largely influenced by our families of origin, where neither of us had learned how to work through conflict in healthy ways. Often times, I would approach Bernie with an issue I wanted to discuss, which would usually include a criticism of some kind, and he would react defensively. An argument would follow, and as things began to escalate, we would both dig in our heels. We each wanted to explain our positions and show where the other person was wrong. As our anger built up on both sides, the intensity and volume would remind me of the out-of-control anger I grew up with in my childhood home, and fear would kick in, sending me into fight or flight mode. That familiar sense of fear was my cue to exit the premises. I would storm out of the room, flinging one final statement of contempt ("You're impossible! I'm done!") or even physically leave the house. Though I was not in physical danger, my emotional safety felt threatened. In those moments, protecting myself from further pain was my number one priority.

Our dynamic felt unworkable, even impossible. One afternoon, as I was playing with the girls upstairs in their bedroom, my stomach twisted in knots when I heard the garage door open, signaling Bernie's return from work. As I anticipated the hundredth round of the same fight, I remember thinking, *This is it. This is where people walk away and call it quits.* Our dream marriage had become a real-life nightmare, and at our lowest point, I wanted out. I wanted peace. I questioned God's providence in bringing us together. *God, what were you thinking? Bernie is from Mexico. I am from northern Michigan. Why on earth did you ever allow our paths to cross? We are the worst possible combination of people you could have put together! We are a million miles away from being the people and the couple we want to be, and we are bringing out the worst in each other.*

As much as I would have loved to wave a magic wand and change Bernie (and the way he expressed his anger), I realized that we both needed to find ways to create safety in our relationship. I also needed to do the hard work of examining my own reactive behaviors. As I began to unpack how my past was influencing my present way of communicating (with the help of a Christian counselor), it made sense that I felt scared during our heated conflicts. Anger was a scary emotion for me—it always had been. I had not understood, however, what Bernie was experiencing during these conflicts. Again, with the help of my counselor, I discovered that underneath his anger, Bernie was just as scared as I was, but for different reasons. Bernie grew up feeling like he had to perform well to be loved, so he feared rejection and abandonment. He couldn't stand the way it felt when I pulled away from him. For him, staying engaged— even in an out-of-control conflict—felt safer to him than me walking away.

Not all couples engage in the pursue/withdraw dance like we do. Not all couples fight and get loud. Bernie and I have walked alongside many couples seeking healing over the years, and we've seen how silence and unhealthy withdrawal can create distance and emotional pain in marriage. Stuffing feelings, turning to addictions, and sweeping problems under the rug can be just as destructive to a relationship as contemptuous fighting.

The truth is, we all have these gaps—these discrepancies between who we want to be and who we really are. And the life and health of our families have *everything* to do with how we handle them.

When our own marriage began to crumble, I couldn't help but feel like we were repeating my first family's story; it was like watching a remake of an old movie. As much as we didn't want to, Bernie and I had co-created our own gap; the ideal of who we *wanted* to be as a couple and as a family did not match the reality we were living. Our foundation of faith was strong, but the house we were building was unstable and had serious problems. Our commitment to stay together had kept us from considering divorce, but merely staying together, even for the sake of our children, was too small a goal. If we wanted a different ending to our story, we were going to have to do some things differently. If we wanted to keep our family intact, we needed to pay attention to what was happening in our marriage. We needed to get help.

The first night we walked into a marriage workshop at our church, I felt like a failure. I never imagined we would need marital help. Maybe that was one of my biggest problems heading into marriage. There was no room in my black-and-white thinking for conflict and struggle in a normal marriage. After filling out a registration form and being assigned to a table with other couples, we quickly discovered we were not alone. We met other couples who were struggling just like us, and there was no judgement.

The teaching that night was from John 5:1-8:

Some time later, Jesus went up to Jerusalem for one of the Jewish festivals. Now there is in Jerusalem near the Sheep Gate a pool, which in Aramaic is called Bethesda and which is surrounded by five covered colonnades. Here a great number of disabled people used to lie—the blind, the lame, the paralyzed. One who was there had been an invalid for thirty-eight years. When Jesus saw him lying there and learned that he had been in this condition for a long time, he asked him, "Do you want to get well?"

What an odd question. The man had been crippled for thirty-eight years, and Jesus asks him if he wants to get well. The man's response is equally surprising:

"Sir," the invalid replied, "I have no one to help me into the pool when the water is stirred. While I am

trying to get in, someone else goes down ahead of me."
(verse 7)

Notice the man doesn't answer Jesus' question. He
explains *why* he can't get into the pool, that there is no one
to help him. Maybe he's lost hope. Maybe he's making
excuses. Maybe he has become so accustomed to being sick
that he doesn't know if he even wants to get well.

> Then Jesus said to him, "Get up! Pick up your mat and
> walk." At once the man was cured; he picked up his
> mat and walked. (verse 8)

Jesus healed the man. Jesus is able and wants to heal us
too. But sometimes, the first question we need to answer is,
"Do we want to get well?" Some of us have been in our
present conditions for a long time. We have been stuck in
the same cycles and repeating the same unhealthy patterns
for years. Are we willing to take the necessary steps to find
freedom from our addictions, to change destructive patterns,
to begin the healing process? Are we willing to humble
ourselves and ask for help? Or, have we become so
comfortable in our brokenness that change sounds too hard?

Bernie and I had to answer that question for ourselves and
for our marriage. We *did* want to get well, and we were
willing to begin the process towards growth and healing. We
recognized that our excuses of, "This is just the way that I
am," and, "The problem isn't me, it's my spouse," were
keeping us on our mats, like the invalid. We didn't have
anyone to help us into the pool because, up until that night,
we didn't want anyone to see how crippled we really were.
We began to open up with our leaders and our group and
be honest about what was really going on. The biblical
teaching and relational skills that were taught from the stage
each week began to transform us from the inside out.

We learned ways to deescalate conflict. We've practiced making requests instead of criticizing, taking ownership rather than reacting defensively, and calling for a time-out when things get too heated. One of the hardest things I've had to learn is how to hang in a little longer when I feel like running away, to stay in the room long enough to say to Bernie, "I need to take a break, but I'm not going anywhere. I love you, and you are a good guy. We'll come back and talk about this after we've cooled off." My instinct to storm out of the room at times is so strong, but when I can reassure Bernie, especially in my anger, that I love him and am for him, it's like poking a hole in a balloon. It deflates the intensity of the conflict. Similarly, it has not been easy for Bernie to learn how to give me the time and space I need to cool down and process what I am thinking and feeling. He has worked hard to sit in the discomfort of us momentarily not being OK, understanding that we both need safety in order to continue a difficult conversation or work through a disagreement.

Bernie was diagnosed with MS shortly after we started the marriage workshop, and his illness put additional strain on our already fragile relationship. Initially, his diagnosis brought us closer together, but as our fears and anger began to surface, we found ourselves more stuck than ever. We sought out skilled counselors as well as highly specialized doctors, and we didn't stop until we found the help we needed. Sometimes, when I suggest counseling to someone, he or she will say, "Oh, we tried counseling once and it didn't work." That is like saying, "I tried a haircut once, but the stylist messed it up, so I haven't gotten a haircut ever again." We once had a counselor tell us, "I don't think I can help you," so we kept looking until we found someone who could. At the end of our first session with our new counselor, he said, "My wife and I have been where you are. There is hope. I can help you." Various doctors have prescribed different medications over the years in order to find the best therapeutic combinations for Bernie's symptoms. Getting the right kind of help is often a process of trial and error, so it's important to not give up. We need to keep praying for direction, seeking help, and asking God to lead us until we find the support and healing we need.

Additionally, we have chosen to live vulnerably in community with other people. This is not easy. We all have the choice to hide and isolate during hard times, or to reach out and let others know we are struggling. We belong to a couple of groups where we can be real about what is going on at home. We have friends who are for us and our marriage. Many years ago, when the girls were very young, Bernie and I got into one of our most heated fights. It was almost midnight, the girls were in bed, and my fear and panic sent me into flight mode. I ran out of the house in my pajamas, without my purse, jumped into the car and drove off, not knowing where to go. I decided to go to my friend Margie's house which was about twenty minutes away. I was already on the tollway when I realized I had no money to pay the tolls. With tears streaming down my face, all I could think about was what a disaster my life and our marriage was. I just needed a safe place to land.

Margie and Dwight were some of the first people we met when we moved to the Chicago area, and we had been in a small group with them for a number of years. More importantly, we had walked through some really difficult times together. They answered the door, welcomed me in, and then Margie and I sat on the couch while I poured out my heart. She listened. She prayed with me. She gave me a safe space to calm down and get my bearings. I returned home early that morning, got a few hours of sleep, and Bernie and I did our best to give each other space and not engage in more conflict that day. Later that afternoon, the doorbell rang: it was a delivery guy with a bouquet of beautiful flowers. When we opened the card, it said, "Bernie and Becky, we are on your side. Love, Margie and Dwight."

It is not difficult to find people who will sympathize with us in our pain, take our side when we complain about our spouse, and say, "Your husband sounds like a real jerk. You don't have to put up with that." Or, "Wow, your wife is a real piece of work. Marriage is the worst." But to find friends who will listen, empathize, but not jump to conclusions is a rarity. To find friends who will speak the truth and point us to the One who can change and heal and transform our mess into something beautiful: that is a priceless gift. We need others who are for us and for our marriage. And we need to be those kind of friends to the married couples in our lives.

Growing our marriage has not been easy and we may always have some gaps, but we have learned we do not have to do it alone. We *cannot* do it alone. In our daily commitment to our marriage and to one another, we are learning how to dance differently. If we want healthier, happier marriages, we have to make them a priority and move them to the front burner. We have to put in the time and effort to learn how to pursue and withdraw in ways that create safety and lead to intimacy. If we do not interrupt our unhealthy ways of dancing and learn new steps, our hearts will harden. And hard hearts will not bring about the marriage we desire or the righteousness that God desires.

Jesus has the healing we need. I no longer question God's wisdom in bringing Bernie and me together, because I see how he uses the brokenness in our marriage to heal the wounds of our past. I see how he uses our story to help others. And I see how he uses disappointments and unfulfilled expectations to draw me to himself. In marriage, God invites us into his work of redemption.

True healing is always precipitated by a genuine desire to get well. It demands that we each do the hard work of owning our gaps and calls for an all-out, radical commitment to the process of transformation by God's grace. A process, by definition, is not immediate. It is a series of actions and steps requiring patience and perseverance. Marriage is a long road, a life-long journey, because sometimes it takes a lifetime to learn how to really love someone.

Four Sets of Five Words

Place me like a seal over your heart,
like a seal on your arm;
for love is as strong as death,
its jealousy unyielding as the grave.
It burns like blazing fire, like a mighty flame.
—Song of Solomon 8:6

I love talking with the young people in my life about relationships and marriage. My daughters, their friends, my nieces and nephews are curious. They want to understand how relationships work. Occasionally, they will ask me some of their burning questions, such as, "Do you believe in 'the one'? Do you think there is one person out there just for you—you know, your soul mate?" Some of the young people I know have grown cynical. They've told me they do not want to get married because they don't want to ever go through a divorce. And they certainly don't want their children to ever experience the pain of a broken home. They see the two as a package deal: divorce as the inevitable end to a marriage doomed from the start.

For those who don't see marriage in their future, when I've asked if they want to have children, some have said they will adopt a baby and be a single parent. The idea of raising a child alone seems more feasible than making a marriage work and avoiding divorce. They've heard the statistics on how many marriages end in divorce, and more significantly, they've lived it. Many of them, having grown up in Christian homes, have experienced the reality of these statistics, and they wonder why. *I wonder why.*

The best answer I can give is that across the board, marriage is hard for most of us. And Christians don't get a pass when it comes to the pain and brokenness we all carry with us into our marriages. Christians aren't immune to the hardships, illnesses, addictions, anxiety, depression, temptations, isolation, and pain most couples experience at some point in marriage. Not only do we all struggle with these things, but we may also feel the pressure and need to pretend that we don't. We are supposed to be an example to those around us. We think others expect us to have it all together. We are called to be salt and light, and when we fall short, fail, and do things Christians aren't supposed to do, we hide. We feel ashamed, and because of our shame, we can't bear the thought of anyone knowing the truth. We put on a smiling face at church, we post our happy family pictures on social media, and we feel like hypocrites because no one really knows what is going on behind closed doors.

If we want to break the cycles and patterns of relational brokenness and shame, we need to be honest and vulnerable. We need to normalize our struggles and let our kids see us bravely ask for help. We must resist every urge to hide and pretend, and instead, own up to our shortcomings. We see the gaps in our families between where we want to be and where we are. Our kids live in those spaces. When we do not reconcile these discrepancies and talk about the fault lines running through our relationships and our families, we set our kids up for disillusionment.

Sometimes we forget that marriage was *God's* idea. He created it for our good, and I want the young people in my life to know that God has a purpose in marriage. In both the good and the hard seasons, he wants to heal us, transform us, and teach us how to really love. He wants us to learn to rely on his strength and look to him for all our needs. And he gives our children a front-row seat as he does his redemptive work.

When we marry, we choose to become family with our spouse for the rest of our lives. I've told my daughters, "I hope that on your wedding day you are crazy in love with your husband. I hope you feel like no other couple on the planet has anything close to the amazing love you've found in each other. And, I also pray that when those feelings fade—and they will—and when hard times come—and they will—that you will not be surprised. There will be times when loving your spouse will be as easy as breathing. You won't even have to try. And there will be times when loving him will be the hardest, most sacrificial thing you've ever done. In fact, you won't be able to do it on your own. You will hurt each other more than you can imagine, and you will need God's help to forgive. When you say, 'I do,' you are signing up for a life-long journey of transformation. You are pledging to love each other through the good and the bad, the best and worst of times, whatever comes your way, for the rest of your lives."

In his book *Sacred Marriage*, author Gary Thomas writes, "The beauty of Christianity is in learning to love, and few life situations test that so radically as does a marriage. . . . If we view the marriage relationship as an opportunity to excel in love, it doesn't matter how difficult the person is whom we are called to love; it doesn't even matter whether that love is ever returned. We can still excel at love. We can still say, 'Like it or not, I'm going to love you like nobody ever has.'"[7]

I speak up in defense of marriage because I believe it is where God does some of his most holy, transforming work. And I tell my kids triumphant stories of people who have persevered in love, people like my friend, Bob.

I met Bob and Jan several years ago at my workplace. Even though they were thirty years my senior, we hit it off right away. (I have a soft spot for people with more wisdom, life experience, and gray hair than me.) They had just moved from Florida to Chicago, and although they were happy to be near their son, they missed the warmer climate and their friends back home. Jan seemed to especially miss it, and they both were dealing the best they could with the diagnosis that had prompted the move: Jan was suffering from Alzheimer's. Bob and Jan visited my workplace regularly, and over time, we developed a lovely friendship. Some days were better than others; Jan would greet me warmly and was able to make simple decisions. But other times, Jan didn't seem to know who I was or what we were talking about. On those days, I'd compliment her nail polish color and just let her do the talking. Sometimes she would tell me surprising stories— I'd nod my head as I listened, and Bob would be standing behind her shaking his head and mouthing the words *No – this never happened.* He often had to repeat the same answer to the same question over and over again, and although I could sense the frustration of the situation, their love for one another was apparent. He took care of her. She trusted him.

As the disease progressed, her memory deteriorated to the point that she no longer recognized her husband of nearly sixty years. One afternoon, I heard the chimes on the door signaling a customer, and in walked Bob, alone. I gave him a hug and asked how things were going, and he told me the disease had progressed significantly. Jan was now consistently confused and agitated. He had come in that day just to talk, and in a moment of raw honesty, he unwrapped the burden he was carrying and shared his pain with me. "This disease is horrific. The part-time care giver who has been coming to our home is not enough. Jan will need full-time care very soon, and the cost is overwhelming. I think we need to go back to Florida where it is not so expensive." I could see the heartbreak in his eyes, and of course, there were no words I could say to make it better. All I could do was listen and be his friend.

As he looked out the window of the store, Bob spotted a three-legged dog walking with his owner, and he insisted we step outside to take a closer look. Sure enough, the dog was walking on three legs, and Bob seemed genuinely tickled by this survivor-wonder dog. As he left the shop that day, I affirmed him for the way he lovingly cared for his wife. I told him I would be praying for him and Jan, and for the difficult decisions he was facing. The words may have sounded cliché, but I meant them. I *would* pray for them because it was the only thing I knew to do.

Then, almost as if talking to himself, he said something I did not immediately understand, but would never forget.

"Four sets of five words."

I didn't get it, so I asked him to repeat it.

He looked back at me, his blue eyes filled with tears, expressing the promises he had made a lifetime ago, the values he had lived by for over half a century, the vows he would keep until God called Jan home.

"Four sets of five words. For better or for worse. For richer or for poorer. In sickness and in health. Till death do us part."

And then he was gone, and I was standing speechless.

When most of us make our marriage promises, if we even use these traditional vows, we are usually in a season of better, richer, and health. We are not thinking about what worse and sickness and poorer might look like down the road. When Bernie and I said our vows to one another more than twenty-five years ago, we had no idea that a diagnosis of multiple sclerosis was waiting for him in his future. Staying together as husband and wife requires a commitment to love one another through the best and worst this life brings. It means when we want to quit, we keep going and take the next right step. When our problems are more than we can handle, we humble ourselves and get help. When our hearts get hard, we allow God to soften them. We choose to forgive. We put our spouse first. We choose to love the way we want to be loved, which is the way God has loved us. Four sets of five words—every day we are given opportunities to make good on our promises, to choose to live out these vows we made so long ago.

And in the worse, the poorer, the sickness, and—someday—the death, we are invited to wholeheartedly trust in a God who is always present with us, a God who is always good. The vows we make to love our spouse "till death do us part" come from the heart of our God who has promised to never leave us, to be with us in the best of times and in the absolute worst of times.

"For I am convinced that neither death nor life, neither angels nor demons, neither the present nor the future, nor any powers, neither height nor depth, nor anything else in all creation, will be able to separate us from the love of God that is in Christ Jesus our Lord" (Romans 8:38-39).

Signs of Life

Instead of cursing the darkness,
light a candle for where we're going.
There's something ahead worth fighting for.
—Neil Young

We have several signs in our home with phrases and words that reflect our values around faith and family, except for the purely sarcastic sign in our laundry room that says, "Laundry: loads and loads of fun." I have been collecting these signs for years, and I used to love romantic signs like "All because two people fell in love . . ." and "They lived happily ever after . . ." But the longer we are married, the more I am drawn to snarkier, less fairy-tale-derived phrases. For our 22nd anniversary I bought a sign that says, "The first fifty years of marriage are always the hardest." It hangs in our dining room and has been a fun conversation piece when friends come for dinner.

We have had the sign "Always kiss me goodnight" hanging over our bed for more than fifteen years, but ever since Bernie visited a sleep clinic several years ago and was diagnosed with sleep apnea and severe snoring (which we did not need an expert to confirm), I've been thinking we should change it to something more realistic. I often go to bed a couple of hours after Bernie, and since he wears a C-Pap machine when he sleeps, kissing him goodnight when I climb into bed is both impractical and potentially dangerous. I'd like to change that sign to something like, "Quiet zone: violators will be poked and prodded." Or, "Marriage is like a walk in the park . . . Jurassic Park." Or maybe, "Marriage is our last, best chance to grow up." [8]

Shortly after we moved into our house, when our girls were very young, I chose three verses from the Bible, printed them out, and had them framed. I hung them on the wall of our family room as our "family mission statements," to serve as reminders and guides as we strived to build our family with Christ at the center.

"Love the Lord your God with all your heart and with all your soul and with all your strength and with all your mind"; and, "Love your neighbor as yourself." (Luke 10:27)

Be kind and compassionate to one another, forgiving each other, just as in Christ God forgave you. (Ephesians 4:32)

Fix these words of mine in your hearts and minds; tie them as symbols on your hands and bind them on your foreheads. Teach them to your children, talking about them when you sit at home and when you walk along the road, when you lie down and when you get up. *Write them on the doorframes of your houses and on your gates.* (Deuteronomy 11:18-20, *emphasis mine*)

In terms of my love for signs, I know I am not alone based on the variety and volume of merchandise I see in stores and online. I'm convinced that we love these signs because they give voice to our values. They express in written words what is written on our hearts. And we see from the verse in Deuteronomy that the idea of posting signs in our homes is not entirely modern—people of faith have been doing it for thousands of years.

Even some of the more idealistic signs appeal to our longings for connection, for building strong families, and for creating a home life that is warm and harmonious. The sign in our kitchen says, "Love is spoken here." Several years ago when some friends were visiting, I shared how our daughter, Brenna, who was seven years old at the time, said we should take the sign down, because "there is too much fighting going on in this house!" One of our friends replied, "Well, you should tell your daughter that sometimes love is loud!" We laughed, but I later thought about the truth in his words. Conflict is unavoidable, and though often times we fight because we are selfish and want our own way, we also fight because we care so deeply about one another and our relationships. We feel the urgency to hash it out, fix the problems between us, and get to a better place. In a sense, our conflicts are signs of life. Like a patient's vital signs that measure breath in lungs and blood pumping through veins, our "loud love" demonstrates vitality and shows our relationships are alive. We want to be heard and understood. We want to be loved. We long for acceptance, closeness, intimacy, and connection, even if the road to get there is strewn with clumsy communication and misunderstandings.

Some people say you should not fight in front of your children, and I agree that it can be scary for children to see their parents hurt one another in their anger. But if we don't teach our children how to work through conflict, who will? We will not do it perfectly. So when our children do see us fight, let's make sure they see us make it right. They can learn from us, even as they see us stumble through the process of learning how to resolve conflicts. When damaging words are spoken and feelings are hurt, let's model what it looks like to ask for forgiveness and seek to understand. When relationships are broken, let's teach our children what it looks like to do the repair work. Let's confess our sins to each other and pray for one another, so that we may be healed (James 5:16). As Bernie and I work through conflicts in our marriage and with each of our daughters, they in turn learn how to work through conflicts with one another. Nobody gets to skip out of resolving hurt. Learning to say how we feel, listening to the other person, avoiding words like "always" and "never", not getting defensive, and forgiving one another are not easy tasks, but we get better at it the more we practice.

Our families are worth fighting for. Our marriages are worth our attention. Our children will only benefit from the time and energy we put into making our relationships the best they can be. They may cry when we leave them with a sitter: let's assure them we will come home after dinner and go anyway. They will think it's gross when we kiss our spouse in front of them: let's be affectionate anyway. (Secretly, they love it, because it makes them feel secure.) We may think we don't have the money to get away for a weekend together, just the two of us: let's get creative and figure out a way to work it into the budget. Let's balance out the money, time, and energy spent on our kids by investing some money, time, and energy into our marriages.

Twenty years from now, it will not matter that our children did all the things. It won't matter that they played all the sports and had the nicest clothes and went on all the trips. When we become grandparents and show up *together* at their houses to babysit for our grandkids so they can get away with their spouses and remember why they fell in love in the first place, they will be thankful we made our marriage a priority.

It is the sign hanging at the top of the staircase whose reminder I need the most. I notice it when I'm coming down the stairs with a laundry basket full of dirty clothes. I see it on my way into the kitchen, and its letters grab my attention when I am cleaning my hardwood floors. Its one word carries more weight than all four stanzas of a hymn. *Pray.* I bought it after my grandmother died, as a reminder of her legacy. My grandma was a compassionate, loving, faith-filled woman, and she often ended her conversations with three words of advice—the best advice she had to give. "Pray on it."

As hard as I may try to work towards growth and maturity, I cannot build the kind of marriage and family I've always wanted solely on my own. I do not have all that it takes, in my own strength, to live out the ideal of who I should and *want* to be. Prayer bridges the gap. In my daily pursuits of mothering and marriage-building, in my ongoing quest to love God with all that I am and to love others as myself, and in my commitment to live authentically in community and to walk in truth, I am completely dependent on God and his strength.

So I pray. I pray for protection and provision. I pray for guidance and direction. I ask God to give us courage to be able to take the next right steps and discern where he leads. When I wander and miss the mark, I ask for forgiveness. When hearts are hard, I pray for God to soften them. I confess my sins and struggles and invite others to pray for me. I ask for wisdom, peace, and help in times of trouble. And I give thanks because this, too, is prayer. I thank God for healing, vitality, and signs of life, even when our love does get a little loud.

Review:

In the daily grind of parenting, we often allow our marriages to be pushed to the back burner. But if we don't pay attention to our marriage during these years, we may not have much of a marriage left by the time our kids leave us. Nurturing the friendships we started with our spouses before we got married and had children is essential if we want to build our homes with wisdom and understanding.

Reflect:

1. In what ways do your and your husband's families of origin impact your marriage? In other words, how is your past affecting your present?

2. What does your marriage "dance" look like: Withdraw/pursue, pursue/pursue, withdraw/withdraw? How can you begin to "dance" in ways that are healthy and create safety for both you and your spouse?

3. What steps can you take to invest in your marriage during these years? (For example: regular date nights, weekends away, improve communication/conflict resolution skills, seek the help of a pastor, counselor, or mentor couple...)

Respond:

God, thank you for my husband. Thank you for bringing us together and making us a family. Help us to make our marriage a priority amidst the demands of parenting. We are your children, holy and dearly loved. Help us to clothe ourselves with compassion, kindness, humility, gentleness and patience. Help us to bear with each other and forgive one another as you have forgiven us. And over all these virtues may we put on love, which binds them all together in perfect unity. Amen (Colossians 3:12-14).

#8—Being A Mom Is the Hardest Job in The World

The Hardest Job You'll Ever Love

There will be so many times you feel like you've failed
but in the eyes, heart and mind of your child,
you're Super Mom.
—Stephanie Precourt

During my first several years of motherhood, I ate my breakfast with Oprah most mornings in our family room, and more than once I heard her say, "Being a mom is the hardest job in the world!" Her words seemed to travel through the camera and the cable lines, through my T.V., straight to my heart. *Thank you very much for saying that, Ms. Winfrey. I'm glad somebody noticed.* I craved validation. I needed to know that what I was doing day in and day out mattered. I wanted assurance that my sleep deprivation and eclectic wardrobe (part maternity, part hubby's old flannel shirts) were somehow contributing toward something of value. But—forgive me in advance for saying this—I think the declaration "Being a mom is the hardest job in the world" is a bit dramatic. I mean, I haven't *had* every job in the world, and there are some I would never even be willing to try. Hostage negotiator? No way. Brain surgeon? I don't think so. Alaskan crab fisherwoman? No, thank you. Podiatrist? I can't even.

If I were speaking these thoughts in front of a live audience, this is where I would quite possibly get booed off stage or have tomatoes thrown at me. (Who brings tomatoes with them to an event?) Hear me out: being a mom is indeed *hard*. There is no doubt. I just think we get into trouble when we make sweeping, generalized claims. Being a dad is also hard. And when we say being a mom is the hardest job in the world, which kind of mother are we talking about? Mothers in developed countries undoubtedly have it better than mothers in the most poverty-stricken places in the world, where people are starving to death on a daily basis. Yet, within our borders, we also have moms who are stuck in cycles of poverty or domestic abuse. Being a single mom has got to be considerably harder than being a married mom, unless your marital problems create stress and strain that make your parenting even more difficult. Being a mom of a child with special needs is understandably harder than being a mom of a healthy child, and moms who suffer from depression, anxiety, or a chronic physical illness clearly have it harder than moms who enjoy good physical, mental, and emotional health.

For some women, becoming a mom fulfills a dream they have had since they were little girls playing with dolls. For other women, being "motherly" does not come naturally. They feel out of their element and are plagued with constant doubts about their ability to mother their child well. Some women adore the baby stage, while others can't wait until their children become more independent so they can regain some freedom. Stay-at-home moms experience exhaustion, isolation, and burn-out. They often miss their careers and crave connection with other adults. They may miss having a "regular" job with meetings and performance reviews and paychecks—anything to show the results of their labor. Moms who work outside the home also experience exhaustion, isolation, and burn-out. They feel the pressure of juggling their work life with their home life, and often times feel they aren't pulling off either job particularly well. And moms in both scenarios often carry hefty burdens of mom guilt. Do you see what I mean? There is just no way to quantify whose job is the hardest, and I do not think it is wise for us to go down that road.

Even if we can't all agree that being a mom is the *hardest* job in the world, I think we can agree on the following truths:

- **Being a mom is the toughest job you'll ever love**. Every mom has her own motherhood journey, meaning that differing aspects and seasons of motherhood are harder for some of us than for others. We each face challenges unique to us, our children, and our families, and some of us struggle in chronic ways that make the daily work of motherhood especially challenging. At the same time, being a mom is also a high calling, a privilege, a chance to grow up and be a kid again all at once, an immensely rewarding endeavor, an ongoing investment, and for me, one of the very best things in my life.

- **Moms are irreplaceable**. The role of mothers in the lives of their children, in our families, in societies, and in our world is unequivocal. No one can ever replace Mom. I have been speaking to groups of moms for more than ten years, and I continue to hear many of them say their greatest fear is that they are not a "good enough mom." They worry they are going to mess up their kids, and in their worst moments they fear that their kids would be better off with a different mom—with a *better* mom. I tell these women what I believe with my whole heart to be true: "You aren't a perfect mom—no one is. But you are *your* kid's mom and the only mom they want. And, of course, you are going to mess up your kids! We all will, in varying degrees and in different ways. But in the messing up that we do, there is a putting back together that only God can do. In an upside-down, backwards, beautiful sort of way he continually teaches us—moms and kids alike—that he is the only one who is good enough. He is enough for us, and he is enough for our kids. Moms, in all your perfect imperfections, you are irreplaceable.

- **Moms need validation.** Motherhood is a uniquely challenging job in that our clients' needs are constantly changing, we are on call 24/7, and somedays we hardly even get a bathroom break. We rarely hear "thank you," and without evaluations, paychecks, or raises, it is very difficult to know whether we are "not meeting, meeting, or exceeding expectations" on any given day.

  When the girls were little, I *despised* having to unbuckle them from their car seats and take them into the store. Especially in the winter. And especially when they were sick. I adored drive-thru coffee shops, restaurants, bank machines, pharmacies—any establishment where I could purchase what I needed without getting out of my car. When picking up a prescription for one of the girls, I would often try to convince the pharmacy employees working at the drive-thru to sell me some children's pain medicine or cough syrup. I'd beg them to sell me a package of diapers. "I wouldn't ask if it wasn't important, but we just came from the doctor, and my daughter has strep throat. I don't want to have to take her out of the car in her sickly state and these arctic conditions . . ." They would politely—and repeatedly—explain to me that they could not sell me any products through the pharmacy drive-thru window. It was strictly for prescriptions.

One time, I actually tried to return a package of ladies' underwear at the pharmacy drive-thru. Oh, I understand that the bigger issue was that I was buying my undergarments at the drug store in the first place. Trust me, it wasn't my first choice; I had purchased them on a day when I had to drag my feverish children into the store in the middle of a blizzard to pick up some diaper cream because the drive-thru attendant refused to sell me any through the window. On my way to the baby care aisle I passed the ladies underwear. I *needed* new underwear and it seemed serendipitous at the time. As it turned out, they weren't really my style or size, so on my next visit to the drug store I tried to return them. I didn't care that the attendant was a young college student—and I knew before I even made the ridiculous request that he would say no. But I was too desperate to be embarrassed. I just needed to run my errands and get my kids home. On days like that, I needed my efforts to count for something. I wanted someone to notice how hard I was trying. I needed validation.

Many years ago, when my aunt Carol was visiting, she validated the work I was doing as a young mom in the most beautiful way. My daughters were preschoolers at the time, and I wanted nothing more than to sit with a cup of coffee and have a meaningful conversation with my aunt, who is one of my most favorite people on the planet. Kate spilled her Cheerios, and I had to help her clean them up. Claire grabbed one of Kate's monkeys from her Barrel of Monkeys set, causing a squabble, and then a pungent odor filled the air signaling that Claire needed her diaper changed. I couldn't even form complete sentences, much less have a coherent conversation, and as my aunt watched the chaos, taking it all in, she was mentally transported back to her own child-rearing days. She exhaled and said, almost to herself, "Gee, when they are little like this, it really is all about survival, isn't it?" I have *never* forgotten that. She could have been frustrated that she had come all that way to visit and we couldn't even get through a conversation. She could have been annoyed that I wasn't paying attention to her. Instead, she remembered her days of nursing bras and poopy diapers. She identified with me right where I was, and she validated the work I was doing. Moms who are further along on this journey are uniquely able to validate moms who are still in the trenches.

- **We do things that make our job harder than it needs to be.** We constantly compare ourselves to others. We measure ourselves up against moms who seem to be more patient, spiritual, fit, and fun, and we feel "less-than." What happens to your joy level when you spend ten minutes scrolling through social media? Most of us tend to share only our prettiest, loveliest moments with the virtual world, and in doing so, we paint a picture that is not reality. When was the last time you were in the middle of a really awful moment, maybe a fight with your husband or a melt-down with your child (either you or the child melting down), and thought, *Everyone hold it! Where's my phone? I need to capture this moment in a photo and post it on Instagram!* Of course, we wouldn't do that. We share the highlights, and then we make up stories in our heads that all the other people out there are only experiencing lovely moments and highlights.

  Isolation also makes our job infinitely harder than it needs to be. Too often, we try to do this motherhood gig on our own. Like a four-year-old striving for independence, we insist, "I can do it all by myself!" Except we can't. So we hide our struggles and pretend we are OK when we are not. As a result, we feel alone. But we were never created to do this alone! We were created to walk together, to bear one another's burdens when the load is too heavy, and to live in authentic, connected relationship with others.

As moms, we may need to redefine our job description, because we tend to think it all depends on us. We believe we are responsible for how things go, how our kids turn out, and how people perceive us and our families. One of the hardest things about being a mom is not being able to control everyone and everything around us. However, when we realize we are partnering *with* God to parent our children, our roles as moms get straightened out and redefined. He is Creator. He is in charge. He is the boss. He is the author of the story. He is the head chef—and like good sous chefs, we do prep work, imitate, and support the work of our Master, asking every step of the way, "Like this, Chef? Is this right, Chef? Does this look good, Chef?" He, in turn, instructs, teaches, affirms, and corrects as we respond, "Yes, Chef!" He oversees and takes responsibility for the outcome. He is shaping us while he shapes our kids, parenting each of us perfectly. I guess technically that would make *his* job the hardest job in the world, except nothing is difficult for him.

All The Things I Forgot
to Tell You

If parenthood came with a GPS
it would mostly just say: recalculating.
—@Simoncholland on Twitter

For all the repeated "I've told you a million times to . . ."
things we say to our children, there are countless words left
unsaid: pieces of advice we don't realize they will need,
surprising things we never could have anticipated or
imagined would occur to them to do, and things they don't
do that we fully expected they would just innately know they
were supposed to do.

When Brenna was four years old, I came down the stairs
a minute after the kitchen timer went off, alerting me that the
cupcakes I had made were done baking. I knew Brenna had
pushed the timer's button, turning it off, but I was shocked
when she announced she had taken the cupcakes out of the
oven. She said it as if it were the most natural, reasonable
thing a four-year-old could have done. Thank God she
properly used oven mitts and didn't burn herself! I was
stunned at my youngest daughter's boldness: I don't think it
would have occurred to my older daughters at that age to do
something I had not instructed them on or specifically told
them to do.

One afternoon, when Claire was six years old, we were
driving back home after picking up my niece in Indiana. After
a lengthy period of silence, I heard Claire's sweet voice from

the back of the minivan, "Mommy, don't get mad at what I'm about to tell you (which is a universal prompt for mothers everywhere to instantly feel both angry and scared). I did something bad." She then confessed that she had taken a couple of beads off of her bracelet and stuck one in each ear, pushing them deep into her ear canals. Even though I had never specifically told her not to put beads in her ears, at six years old, she knew this was a bad idea. But she had recently seen a show about spy kids, and she just wanted to know what it would be like to have a spy earpiece in each ear.

After a visit to the pediatrician who successfully removed one bead, and then a visit to the ear, nose, and throat doctor who was able to remove the stubborn second bead in less than thirty seconds, we drove home in silence. Claire was embarrassed. The second doctor scolded her pretty severely for doing something she surely knew better than to do (although I can't imagine he was too bothered when our insurance paid a hefty bill for the "surgical procedure" he performed). I couldn't really blame her for her curiosity or severe lapse in judgement, because when I was around her age, I swallowed three copper pennies from my red, long-handled Dairy Queen spoon while my older sister stood in the doorway of my bedroom and watched. She was absolutely horrified. To this day, I don't know why I did it. I was curious. My brain was momentarily hijacked by some kind of impulsive, creative inspiration. And, in my defense, no one ever told me not to eat coins.

One of Brenna's first softball coaches loves to tell the story of the first day we dropped her off at the field. She was in third grade, and we had registered her last minute because her interest in playing was very last minute—she wanted to play with her friend who had also signed up. We scrambled to get her a youth-sized glove and barely got to the field in time for her first practice. There had been no time for going over basic softball skills. We hadn't even played catch with her or showed her how to hold a bat. Coach lined the girls up on one side of the field, and going down the line, he introduced himself to each girl, asked her name, and tossed the ball to her. Brenna was not really paying attention, and when he got to her, he tossed the ball to her just like he had to the other girls, fully expecting her to catch it—or at least attempt to catch it. But Brenna just stood there with her arms at her sides, her glove on the wrong hand, and didn't even flinch as the ball came sailing towards her face. The ball hit her on the forehead, and the coach, stunned in disbelief, immediately ran to see if she was OK. A lump was already forming on her forehead, which Brenna emphatically insisted had always been there. He later joked that she was the most improved player that first season, considering her growth from that first day of practice to their last game. Coach never let her (or us) live that down.

We do our best to teach our kids the important stuff of life. And as moms, we are also trying to do what *we've* been told—the checklist we have in our minds for how to be a good parent:

- Read to your kids.
- Play at the park.
- Feed them organic fruits and veggies.
- Be involved.
- Don't be a helicopter parent.
- Talk about sex.
- Talk about drugs and alcohol.
- Talk about Jesus.
- Talk about stranger danger.
- Don't talk too much.
- Be a good listener.
- Be the parent, not the friend.
- Be fun!
- Limit screen time.
- Limit sugar.
- Have regular family dinners.

- Have regular family devotions.
- Try harder.
- Do better.

In all these "to dos," there may be some things we have forgotten—some truths we haven't heard in a while that our loving Father wants to speak over us. We spend so much time focusing on what we should *do*; he wants us to focus on who he *is*. And if we quiet ourselves and listen, he wants to remind us who we are as his beloved children. He says:

- You are loved. (1 John 3:1)
- My perfect love drives out your fears. (1 John 4:18)
- My grace is enough for you. (2 Corinthians 12:9)
- I forgive all your sins. (Psalm 103:12)
- There is no condemnation for those who belong to me. (Romans 8:1)
- My mercies are new every morning. (Lamentations 3:22-23)
- I am trustworthy. (Psalm 100:5)
- I have good plans for you and your children. (Jeremiah 29:11)
- I satisfy you like nothing else—and no one else—ever could. (John 4:13-14)
- My strength is made perfect in your weakness. (2 Corinthians 12:9)
- Nothing is too difficult for me. (Jeremiah 32:17)
- I constantly watch over your life and the lives of your children. (Psalm 121:7-8)
- I am able to do immeasurably more than you could even think or imagine. (Ephesians 3:20)
- Nothing can separate you from my love. (Romans 8:38-39)
- You are mine. (Isaiah 43:1)

Fly, Birdie, Fly

A bird in a nest is secure,
but that is not why God gave it wings.
–Matshona Dhliwayo

Knowing when to push our kids—and when to back off—is one of the hardest aspects of parenting. One year, our family went zip lining at summer camp, and our youngest daughter, Brenna, was totally on board—right up until the last moment when she lost her courage. I knew she really wanted to do it, so I told her older sister, Kate, to go with her and push her, if necessary. She needed the push! Her initial screams of terror turned into squeals of delight once her feet touched the ground. "Mommy, I want to go again!"

We've all heard the parenting analogy of the mama bird pushing her baby birds out of the nest. The baby birds won't leave on their own—they don't even know they can fly! This is why at precisely the right moment, which the mama bird knows because of her amazing motherly intuition, she gives them a push. I have just a few questions about this terrifying process. What if your baby birds are overly confident and do think they can fly, but as the mama bird you know they aren't ready? Or maybe you're the one who isn't ready? Or what if your motherly intuition isn't working properly and you push them out too soon? What goes through the poor birds' minds as their mother displaces them from the only home they've ever known, hurling them toward the ground? And who pushes the mama bird when she isn't ready to push her babies? To push, or not to push, that is the question!

I started stuttering in third grade, and school quickly became the most difficult part of my life. By the time I got to middle school, the stuttering and related anxiety were so severe that I had chronic stomach issues and trouble sleeping at night. Some teachers were compassionate and understanding of my struggle; others, sadly, were not. One teacher in particular called on me repeatedly to answer questions and read out loud in class, even after my mother spoke with him and asked him to stop. Most days, I'd come home after school and lay on the couch in tears because of the humiliation I experienced with teachers and students alike. If homeschooling had been an option during those years, I would have begged my mom to do it. I dreaded going to school each day.

My mom knew not to push me. She knew that going to school each day and dealing with teachers who continued to call on me—and classmates who laughed at me—was almost more than I could take. When I was at home, she didn't push me to do things that were hard. She didn't make me answer the phone. She didn't force me to go to youth group when I was afraid I'd have to speak in front of everyone. She ordered for me in restaurants. She went back to school and talked to my teacher again and insisted that he stop calling on me. She would sit next to me on the couch and rub my back. She would tell me she was sorry it was so hard and that she loved me. As my mom, she knew that was what I needed most.

Some of our children are experiencing tremendous pressure. They feel pressure to perform, to fit in, to look a certain way or hit a certain number on the scale, to be in advanced classes, to get perfect grades, and to make the team. Their value and identity and worth as a human being can easily get wrapped up in what they do, and if we don't pay attention as parents, we can unknowingly heap even more pressure on these children we love so much. We don't even know we are doing it, because too often our value and identity and worth as human beings are wrapped up in what *we* do.

Sometimes our kids need to be pushed. Sometimes they need external motivation to take necessary steps forward or keep a commitment they made. Sometimes they need to borrow courage from us to do the things they really want to do, even though they are afraid. These are the times we push. And if it's too hard, we invite other mama birds to help us gently nudge our little birdies when we can't do it on our own. We borrow courage from our brave friends who have more experience, wisdom, and broader perspectives than we do.

Other times, we see the way our children are struggling. We see how they are giving all they can to get through the day, and we know that when they come home the last thing they need is to be pushed. They are desperate for a soft space to land. They need to rest and breathe. They long to just *be*. They need us to remind them that their worth does not come from what they do—that they are loved just as they are. The day will come when they will be ready. But today is not that day.

E for Effort

Being a mom has made me so tired. And so happy.
—Tina Fey

If I were to be graded on my performance as a mom, I would want the grade to be based on results plus effort. I would want my good intentions factored into the final score. Forevermore, I would like it to be known that I did the best I could with what I knew at the time. I'll admit, my thinking is a little messed up as it relates to performance and motherhood. While we aren't officially graded on how well we do as moms, I am regularly conducting self-evaluations and performance reviews, and the marks consistently fall somewhere between "meets expectations" and "needs improvement." Occasionally—though not very often—I'll come through an experience feeling really good about how I handled things, or I'll have a great moment of connection with one of my daughters, and when I lay my head on my pillow at the end of the day, I enjoy the fleeting satisfaction of a job well done. I give myself a solid "exceeds expectations" before drifting off to sleep.

But more often, when my head hits the pillow, I feel a bit deflated and discouraged. I thank God for his help and grace that covers what I cannot, but I end many days thinking, *Parenting is hard. Moms all around me seem to be nailing it. Everyone else seems to have this figured out. What is wrong with me?*

When Kate went off to college, our sometimes-strained relationship seemed to improve almost instantly. We have always been very close, and in some ways we are a lot alike:

strong-willed, introverted, and fearful of rejection. We are both a six on the Enneagram. We crave approval and acceptance. We get stuck in our heads a lot, and conflict is something we can stumble into rather easily. Those first few weeks of her being away at school were a mixed bag of emotions. I missed her. I was trying to get used to my new role in her life as a hands-off parent. We texted often and FaceTimed a couple of times a week, and we verbally offered our appreciation to one another. Even though it was a difficult adjustment, I found myself thinking, *This could be good.*

Our first visit was family weekend, the third week of September. It seemed like a million people descended on campus that weekend, so we decided to spend time together as a family off campus, heading into Grand Rapids for their annual Art Prize festival. We arrived Friday evening and immediately presented Kate with all the goodies we brought for her: a couple of twin air mattresses and an air pump for friends to use when they came to visit, various pantry and beauty products she had requested, some spackle for the walls (she said, "Don't ask!"), and a few home cooked meals for her freezer. Then, we headed out for dinner. It was so good to be together, and as Bernie and I walked behind our three girls, watching them catch up and laugh and enjoy their sister-bond, I commented that Kate seemed full of joy. She appeared to be more carefree than when she was at home and had made a lot of friends in the short time she had been at school. My heart swelled with love and joy watching her in her element. She was thriving.

The weekend went downhill from there. After dinner that night, Claire got the worst case of stomach flu of her life. She threw up all night and slept all day at the hotel on Saturday. The weather was unseasonably and unbearably hot, which made the swarms of people even harder to tolerate. Kate and I hiccupped our way through the day, testy and irritable with one another, managing to miscommunicate and offend each other repeatedly. As we walked around campus, I saw mothers and daughters everywhere I looked, and none of them seemed to be having a hard time. It was family weekend for crying out loud! Why couldn't we enjoy our time together? Why couldn't we just be normal like everyone else? I remembered how happy and carefree Kate had seemed a day earlier, and I couldn't help but think that the tension and irritation that now hung between us must have been my fault.

On Sunday morning we grabbed some breakfast, and after hanging out for a while in the common area of Kate's building, we were ready to hit the road and head back to Chicago. Kate's birthday was coming up the following weekend, and I had it in my head that we should decorate her door with a birthday banner before we left. I wanted everyone to know it was her birthday, especially since I wouldn't be there to do our usual birthday fanfare (which is actually very simple and low-key). Kate knew something was up when Bernie and I hung back while the girls made their way towards the stairwell, and when she realized we were taping a birthday banner on her door, she was less than appreciative.

"What are you doing? I don't want everyone to know it's my birthday! You should know that I don't like drawing attention to myself." She was visibly upset, and I was understandably hurt. I was just trying to do something nice for my daughter. And I had it in my head that decorating her dorm door with a birthday banner was what a good mother would do for her college daughter's first birthday away from home. After all, a good friend of mine (who happens to be a phenomenal mom) had recently decorated their garage door with a huge "Sweet Sixteen" banner when her daughter got her driver's license, and I was just trying to be a good mom.

Kate now admits that she was being difficult that weekend. And I am not saying that as her mom I should have been able to read her mind in terms of what would have been the perfect way to acknowledge her birthday. But the truth is, if I had stopped to think for one minute about the fact that Kate absolutely *hates* being the center of attention, I would have realized that decorating her door was not something she would have wanted. She doesn't even allow us to sing Happy Birthday to her in a restaurant or ask the waiter to bring a birthday dessert with candles. If I had thought about what would have spoken love to my daughter instead of trying to copy what my friend did for *her daughter*, I would have left flowers and York mints for her in her apartment. If I could go back and do it over, I would have left a card on her pillow filled with words of affirmation because that has always been her love language. People feel loved when they feel known, and my intention to do something special actually caused hurt.

We don't get to go back and do moments over again, but we can move forward, learn from our mistakes, and try again next time. The value we gain, even through our mistakes, is that the more we know, the better we can love. In all of it, perhaps the very hardest part of being a mom is accepting that all of our efforts—however clumsy they may be—are ultimately leading towards one goal: preparing our babies to leave our nest. They will leave our nest, but they will never leave our hearts. And that is, I think, the very best thing about being a mom.

Review:

One of the hardest things about being a mom is not being able to control everyone and everything around us. However, when we realize we are partnering *with* God to parent our children, our roles as moms get straightened out and redefined. He oversees and takes responsibility for the outcomes. He is shaping us while he shapes our kids, parenting each of us perfectly. So that would make *his* job the hardest job in the world, except nothing is difficult for him.

Reflect:

1. Where do you find validation for the hard work you are doing as a mom?

2. Which of the following are you doing that makes your job harder than it needs to be?
    *   Comparing yourself (or your family) to others
    *   Isolating yourself from others
    *   Maintaining a self-sufficient mentality
    *   Trying to control what we cannot

3. Which of the truths listed on page 167 resonate with you the most? How can you meditate on these truths so they become a part of your internal dialogue?

Respond:

God, thank you for the gift of being a mom. Help me to find the validation I need in you. When I am tempted to seek validation elsewhere, compare myself to others, isolate, and rely on my own strength, please show me a better way. Help me to turn to you and find the strength and help I need. When the challenges of motherhood overwhelm me, help me to remember that you are with me. "Ah, Sovereign Lord, you have made the heavens and the earth by your great power and outstretched arm. Nothing is too hard for you" (Jeremiah 32:17). Amen.

#9—Always Trust Your Motherly Instincts

Mirror, Mirror

There is a way that appears to be right,
but in the end it leads to death.
—Proverbs 14:12

As we waited for the attendant to begin boarding our flight, my anxiety continued to increase. I just could not shake the feeling that we should *not* get on that plane. I wasn't sure what the problem was, exactly, but my gut was telling me that if we boarded that plane we would not reach our earthly destination. Maybe it was a mechanical problem of some sort. I saw some uniformed crew members pass by with their bags, and the pilot looked a little glassy-eyed. Maybe that was it! Maybe our pilot was intoxicated or on drugs, and he was going to drive our plane into the ground. Or maybe it was a terrorist. I glanced around at the other passengers, not noticing any suspicious activity. I looked over at my husband, who was checking his email on his phone, and knew he would not understand my sense of impending doom. He is not an intuitive person. I considered my choices: I could refuse to board the plane, but that would create quite an embarrassing situation because my husband would undoubtedly think I was being irrational. (Also, I would most likely upset and confuse my daughters who, at fourteen, twelve, and seven years old would not understand my sixth sense.) Or, I could suck it up, ignore the warning my gut was screaming at me, and get on that plane. I chose the latter, revealing that my fear of embarrassing my husband was slightly greater than my fear of death. As has been true on many occasions, my gut proved me wrong. The only thing wrong on that flight was the food.

I am a catastrophic thinker by nature. If jumping to conclusions was an Olympic sport, I would medal in it. Eight weeks into my pregnancy with our eldest daughter, Kate, I became absolutely convinced I was having a miscarriage. A year earlier, we had lost our first baby right around nine weeks, and when I didn't feel Kate move for several hours, I just knew that history was repeating itself. I called my doctor, sobbing into the phone. She advised me to come in right away for an ultrasound, which showed a healthy, growing baby with a strong heartbeat. I was stunned. I had been so sure that my body and brain were telling me the truth.

A few years later, when I was eight months pregnant with our second daughter, Claire, Bernie woke up early on the morning of our anniversary and went biking. He was supposed to be home in plenty of time for us to go to church, and when he didn't come home, I knew something terrible had happened. As a half hour turned into an hour, and then two, I found myself smack dab in the middle of my worst-case scenario moment. I called the police, and after questioning me in our living room, I begged them to go look for my husband. They wanted to wait it out a bit, suggesting that maybe he had forgotten to buy me an anniversary present and that was why he was running late. It took every ounce of my self-control to not scream, "Just go look for him! He's probably dead in the woods by now, but in case he's still alive, if you leave now maybe you can get to him, before it's too late!" Moments later, I got a call from a number I didn't recognize. It was Bernie. He had gotten a flat tire deep in the forest preserve and had left his phone in the car. *Whoops. Thank you, officers, for your time, but we're good now. Be safe out there.*

Moms whose instincts are working properly can supposedly tell if their child has a fever by kissing her forehead. They can differentiate their baby's hungry cries from their dirty diaper cries. Not me. My milk would let down at the sound of *any* baby crying—even if I was at the grocery store shopping without my kids. Moms with functioning guttural instincts can tell when their kids are lying and know precisely what to do in any given situation. They don't overreact or underreact because they can gauge the appropriate level of concern in each circumstance. They just *know*.

When Kate was in ninth grade, she pretty much locked herself in her room for the whole month of January. My gut told me something was seriously wrong. *She's depressed. She has a secret boyfriend she's not telling us about. Maybe even an older guy who is fish tailing her, or whatever you call it.* I asked her numerous times if everything was okay. I tried to pry some nugget of information out of her when she came home from school or at dinnertime. She kept saying nothing was wrong. Then she started exercising, walking on the treadmill in our basement, which was definitely out of the ordinary.

One day, even though she had specifically told me not to come down to the basement while she was working out (rookie move on her part), halfway through her work-out I descended the stairs to tell her dinner would be ready in fifteen minutes. She had her headphones in, and since the treadmill faced away from the stairs, she didn't hear or see me coming. I unintentionally scared the bejeebies out of her, she slammed her laptop shut, and that day, at 5:35 CST, the mystery was solved. Turns out, she was not depressed or dating a thirty-year-old after all. She had been watching the first nine seasons of *The Office* like it was her job. Thinking that

I wouldn't approve, she decided it was better to ask forgiveness than permission. Kate lost her computer privileges for not following our rules and then hiding it (our rule was that the kids had to get permission before watching TV on their devices), and I felt relieved and slightly amused. Before falling asleep that night, Bernie and I laughed over the misdemeanor offense of our eldest daughter, grateful she wasn't hiding anything more serious from us. We also laughed over my far-fetched suspicions of what she had been up to the entire month of January.

When we talk about "motherly instincts," we really are describing a feeling we get, a "knowing" deep in our gut, a sixth sense of sorts that influences our decision making. But these instincts can easily steer us wrong when they are fueled by guilt, fear, insecurities, or faulty thinking. It can be helpful to explore the following questions: *In my parenting, why do I react the way I do? What is motivating my response in this situation? What are the underlying beliefs behind my thoughts and feelings? Where is my energy around this issue coming from?* Sometimes my reactions are driven not by my child's needs, but rather by *my* needs for security, approval, acceptance, control, or to feel good about myself as a mom.

I fear something bad will happen to my child, so I don't allow her to participate in reasonable, age-appropriate activities. Better to be safe than sorry. My need for safety and security can cause me to be a helicopter mom, hovering over my children in over-protection mode.

When I am driven by my insecurities, I worry others will judge me based on my child's behavior or my parenting decisions. I worry I will be judged because I have been guilty of judging other moms along these lines. The truth is, I don't have control over my child's behavior or what other people think about me and my parenting style. If I allow my child's behavior plus other people's opinions of me as a mom to determine my value and worth, my sense of identity will frequently come under siege. In a moment when my child needs me to teach, correct, or discipline, or in a moment when my child needs me to be tender and hold her in my arms, I may be so worried about what other people are thinking about me that I miss meeting my child's need.

At times, my instincts are skewed by guilt. I lost my temper this morning with my daughter, so this afternoon, I sweep her disobedience under the rug rather than deal with it. I think I am trusting my gut and choosing my battles, but the truth is that letting it go feels better than starting a fight. I can't stand the way it feels to have my child be angry or disappointed with me, so I give in or look the other way.

Our gut feelings are just that—feelings. They may or may not be based in truth. At times my intuition is right on the money. I have a sense that my child is struggling with something, so I ask a couple of good questions in the right moment and my hunch is proved correct. Then, I am able to help my child and show empathy and understanding. But as I've demonstrated, oftentimes my hunches are off. I have been overly suspicious of my teen daughters because I remember some of the things *I* did at their age. Those memories spark my imagination, creating all sorts of ideas about what my children are actually doing on a Friday night. And when I act on those suspicions as if they are true, not only do I miss the mark with my children, but my choices and responses can actually cause harm. I know I am not the only mom who is led astray at times by her emotions, desires, and faulty thinking.

Consider Eve, the very first mother. In her defense, she had no mother to learn from. She had no friends to bounce ideas off of. She wasn't part of a ladies' Bible study or moms' group on Facebook. She had a husband, a garden, and perfect communion with her Creator. We know how the story goes. She is given a choice to obey or disobey God, to follow his commands or follow her gut. She chooses the latter and eats from the one tree that God had specifically said was off-limits. Why does she do it? God had given her and Adam an entire garden filled with fruit trees from which to eat, except for the one tree in the middle. The fruit on that tree was not to be eaten. God had given them immense freedom with one restriction. In the following text, the crafty serpent questions Eve, and immediately we see how he twists God's words.

> He said to the woman, "Did God really say, 'You must not eat from any tree in the garden'?"
>
> The woman said to the serpent, "We may eat fruit from the trees in the garden, but God did say, 'You must not eat fruit from the tree that is in the middle of the garden, and you must not touch it, or you will die.'"
>
> "You will not certainly die," the serpent said to the woman. "For God knows that when you eat from it your eyes will be opened, and you will be like God, knowing good and evil."
>
> When the woman saw that the fruit of the tree was good for food and pleasing to the eye, and also desirable for gaining wisdom, she took some and ate it. She also gave some to her husband, who was with her, and he ate it. Then the eyes of both of them were opened, and they realized they were naked; so they sewed fig leaves together and made coverings for themselves. (Genesis 3:1-7)

When the serpent subtly tries to twist what God had said, Eve corrects him. So then he tries a different approach: he tells her a bold-faced lie. He tells her that what God said is not true. He convinces her that God is withholding good from her. As she considers his words, she can't help but notice how enticing the fruit is. She sees how perfectly ripe it is, and she can almost taste the sweetness of the fruit's flesh. She becomes aware of her desire to gain wisdom and be like God. So she takes and she eats. She gives some to her husband, who has been right there with her, and he also eats it. Their eyes are opened, but not in the way the serpent had predicted. Instead of becoming like God, they become afraid. Instead of being filled with knowledge, they are filled with shame. And in their shame, they hide from God.

Our gut is not a good navigational tool. Faulty thinking and false beliefs will lead us down a path of wrong choices, attempts to cover up those choices, and shame. We are just as vulnerable as Eve—just as easily deceived into disbelieving what God has said and doubting his goodness. We, too, are led astray and enticed by our sinful desires. Temptation's pull is strong, and we simply cannot trust our feelings.

In the account of Sarai and Hagar, we see how Sarai's actions create pain for her and her family. God had promised them a son, but much time had passed, and Sarai had not conceived. So Sarai tells her husband, "The Lord has kept me from having children. Go, sleep with my slave [Hagar]; perhaps I can build a family through her" (Genesis 16:2). Sarai's maternal instinct was strong. I understand the God-given desire to have a baby. I know first-hand the pain of losing a baby and waiting month after month for a dream that refuses to come true. I don't blame Sarai for growing impatient and wanting to take matters into her own hands because I, too, have tried to control that which I cannot. I have grown impatient and weary of waiting for God to answer a prayer.

A generation later we see how Rebekah, Sarai's daughter-in-law, brings similar pain and chaos to her own family by following her own flawed intuition. Rebekah's favoritism for one son over the other leads her to deceive her husband Isaac, taking advantage of his old age and weak eyesight. She comes up with an elaborate plan to help Jacob trick his father into giving the blessing to him, instead of to his twin brother Esau, who was the first-born and his father's favorite. This act of betrayal creates a rift between brothers that nearly results in murder. Jacob flees for his life, and more than twenty years pass before Jacob and Esau are reunited and able to forgive one another. God heals and restores, but what pain we bring on ourselves and on those we love when we rely on our own understanding and go our own way!

Our sinful desires will lead us astray. Our fears and faulty thinking will cause us to act and react in ways that are contrary to what God wants for us, for our children, and for our families. We need friends—godly women—to remind us of what is true and help us see things from a different perspective. And we need wisdom from God, which he promises to generously supply to all who ask (James 1:5).

I can't help but wonder how things may have been different if Eve could have picked up the phone and called a friend, running the serpent's advice by someone who could have reminded her of God's goodness and truth. What if Sarai had checked out her surrogacy idea with a faith-filled friend who could have encouraged her to be patient and to trust God's timing and plan? What if Rebekah had taken a few moments to pray before concocting her devious plan, asking God for wisdom in helping her sons prepare for their father's death?

The good news is that we are not called to instinctively make our way through motherhood on our own, relying on our hunches and feelings. God gives us wise counsel through trusted friends. He has given us his Word to light our path and his Spirit to remind us of what is true. He invites us to trust him from the bottom of our hearts, to rely on his wisdom in every situation.

Trust in the Lord with all your heart
    and lean not on your own understanding;
in all your ways submit to him,
    and he will make your paths straight.

(Proverbs 3:5-6)

Five-Day Free Parenting Trial

I was a wonderful parent before I had children.
—Adele Faber

I took my first crack at parenting when Bernie and I were newlyweds. We enthusiastically agreed to care for our eighteen-month-old niece, Britta, for five days while her parents went out of town. I had grand plans for how those five days would go, and since I was pregnant with our eldest daughter, Kate, I was eager to try out my mothering skills. I had all sorts of ideas and opinions about how to raise children, and I couldn't wait to practice my techniques on my niece.

On our first day together, I strapped Britta into her stroller, and we made our way over to the pool area in our apartment complex. I knew the kiddie pool would be the perfect way to kick off our fun time together. However, as I tried to remove Britta's shoes so we could wade into the water, she fought me. She resisted repeatedly, kicking her feet, but I persisted. I held her tight while I worked on untying her laces. *I'm the grown up here. I just need to be firm. Once she understands what we are doing, she'll get on board.* I finally got her shoes off, in spite of her screams and protests, but as I stood her up and grabbed her hand, she broke free and began to run away from me. She tripped and fell, scraping her feet and legs on the cement. When Britta realized her knee was bleeding, she became even more hysterical. I felt terrible. I cleaned her wounds the best I could with a baby wipe from her diaper bag and put her shoes back on as fast as possible as I tried—

unsuccessfully—to calm her frantic cries. As I pushed the stroller back to our apartment, Britta finally stopped her wailing, but I felt defeated. *Okay, Kid, you win. What kind of mother am I going to be?*

Later, when I told my sister about what had happened, she told me that Britta had a thing about not taking her shoes off. *You don't say. That would have been helpful information.* During my time with Britta, I mistakenly thought I would be calling the shots. I fully expected to nail this pre-parenting challenge and maintain control of every situation, but I quickly realized how much I had to learn.

From the moment they are born, children demonstrate they are individuals with strong characteristics hard-wired into their DNA. Although they inherit certain traits from us and adopt many of our habits and mannerisms, they have their own ideas and opinions about things from a very early age. And while there are some great books to help prepare expectant parents for the challenges they will face, there is no real manual for parenting. In the situation with Britta at the pool, I failed to listen to her as she was communicating with me the only way an eighteen-month-old could have in that moment. Through her cries and protests she was telling me she did not want to go in the pool. And she most certainly did not want to take off her shoes. My preconceived ideas about how that morning was going to go down were challenged and overturned. My instinct to keep going with my plan—to let her know who was boss—backfired because it was not what Britta needed in that moment. It was what *I* wanted, the idea I had in my head of the way things were supposed to go.

Sometimes our expectations need to be adjusted. In moments when things are not going the way we think they should be going, when our children are not behaving the way we want them to behave, and this parenting thing is not going as smoothly as we planned, sometimes we need to surrender our dream and accept our reality. Britta did not want to take off her shoes or go in the pool. She wanted to ride in the stroller. She wanted to watch Barney and cuddle on my lap while I read her books. When I put her to bed that first night, I left her shoes on. They were clunky in her porta crib, and I remember thinking how uncomfortable it would be to wear your shoes while sleeping. Unless, of course, you loved the way it felt to wear your shoes so much that you never wanted to take them off. *Okay, Kid, you win. Thank you for teaching me something about being a mom. I guess we both win.*

Planes, Trains, and Anxiety

The way of fools seems right to them,
but the wise listen to advice.
—Proverbs 12:15

When my in-laws invited our teen daughters to go on a month-long trip to Europe, my excitement quickly turned to anxiety. There were so many things to worry about. *What if something happens when the girls are traveling alone? What if they get homesick? What if they get lost or left behind? What if they fight over their clothes on the cruise ship and one of them pushes the other overboard?* I'll admit, that last one was a tad extreme, but these were the thoughts that kept me up at night. The girls had never been gone for more than a few days at church camp. Kate had some anxiety about traveling and being away from home for such a long time, and my motherly instincts were telling me—shouting at me—that I would have to be crazy to let them go halfway across the world for a month. They were only fifteen and thirteen at the time.

I knew that my "instincts" were driven by fear and were not reliable. My intuition could not be trusted, but my friends could be. So I went to them for the courage I lacked. I reached out to my tribe of women, looking for different perspectives. I asked them to help me see what I couldn't see on my own.

I emailed a mom I knew whose children had traveled extensively. She was delighted over the girls' opportunity to visit Greece, Italy, Turkey, and France. My sister, Kari, understood my fears, but helped me see the relational value of this trip. The girls would get to know their grandparents and their cousin better. They would get to experience this trip as sisters and create memories they would both cherish forever. My friend, Margie, challenged my tendencies to operate from a place of fear, and in my parenting, to rescue and try to shield my children from any type of hardship. She gently reminded me that Kate and Claire would grow through any challenges they would encounter. And they would do it *together*. God would be with them and help them, and I would grow too. God would help me, too.

And my friend, Marla, who is very logical and rationally minded, told me it would be the trip of a lifetime. It would be a chance for the girls to explore and discover new places, food, and culture, and she promised me they would come back alive. I knew it was ridiculous for her to promise me the girls' safe return because it was outside of her control, but she knew I needed to hear it.

I didn't ask these women for their opinions because they were just like me and would tell me what I was already thinking. On the contrary, I went to them because I knew they would have *different* thoughts than mine. My hope was that they would give me what I was lacking: a perspective not fueled by fear. These women helped me be brave. They equipped me to help my children be brave. They helped me rise up and be the mother my children needed me to be.

The girls went on the trip. They saw amazing sights and ate strange and wonderful foods. They created memories with their grandparents and cousin that they will always treasure. They learned to hand-wash their clothes in their tiny bathroom sink. Claire left home a vegetarian and came back eating meat and drinking coffee. Kate, our pickiest eater, tried foods I wouldn't even want to try. And sure enough, while visiting the historical, Biblical town of Ephesus, they had an epic fight over clothes. They survived. I survived. We all grew, and I had the joy of knowing that in this one thing, I did not let my fear call the shots.

My daughters have not only been mothered by me. They have been indirectly mothered by Kari, Margie, Marla, my mom, my aunt, my grandma—women who have helped shape me and have walked with me on my journey. I have borrowed strength from these women again and again, and I've learned that I am a better mother when I let them coach me. None of us has what it takes on our own. None of us is sufficiently well-rounded and grounded to get it right all the time. We need the help of wise friends who know us and know our children. We need other moms in our corner who know our stories—where we've come from and where we are aspiring to go. And we desperately need the truth of God's Word to light our paths, shape our perspectives, correct our faulty thinking, and supply the wisdom we lack.

Review:

When we are driven by our insecurities and fears, led astray by faulty thinking and sinful desires, and when our instincts are skewed by guilt, we react accordingly. Our gut feelings are just that—feelings. They may or may not be based in truth. The good news is that we are not called to instinctively make our way through motherhood on our own, relying on our hunches and feelings. God gives us wise counsel through trusted friends. He has given us his Word to light our path and his Spirit to remind us of what is true.

Reflect:

1. How do insecurities, fears, guilt, faulty thinking, and sinful desires lead you to act and react in ways that are contrary to what God desires?

2. To whom do you turn when you need a fresh perspective? Who is walking with you on this journey, helping you to see things you otherwise wouldn't be able to see?

3. In James 1:5 we are encouraged to ask God for wisdom whenever we need it, with the assurance that he will give it *generously*. How accustomed are you to asking God for wisdom in various parenting situations? How might it impact your parenting if you were to regularly receive generous portions of wisdom in your everyday life as a mom?

Respond:

God, thank you that your Word is a lamp for my feet and a light on my path (Psalm 119:105). I acknowledge there are many times when I go my own way and do what seems right in my own eyes. Help me to seek you and hear your voice. Help me to respond with wisdom rather than react in the moment. I want to trust you with all my heart and lean not on my own understanding; as I submit to you in all my ways, make my paths straight (Proverbs 3:5-6).

#10—You Can Do It All If You Just Try Harder

The Supermom Myth

There is no way to be a perfect mother and a million ways to be a good one.
—Jill Churchill

"Supermoms do exist, and if I try hard enough, I can be one of them!" We may not actually say this one out loud, but most of us have bought into some version of this lie. The unfortunate truth—that many of us discover the hard way—is that no matter how hard we try, we cannot have it all, do it all, and be everything to all people at all times. When we run ourselves into the ground trying to please and impress everyone, we experience depletion and burnout instead of joy and fulfillment. And when we are driven by comparison—fueled by the picture-perfect images we see presented on social media—we often cave under the pressure of trying to create the ideal life we feel we may be missing out on (and then feel guilty and disappointed when we fail). When we try to do everything, especially things that don't align with who we are and how we are uniquely wired, we often feel frustrated that we aren't really excelling in any area in our lives.

At first glance, it may appear that Proverbs 31 is a biblical description of a spiritual Super Woman. (If you've never read this chapter, I encourage you to look it up. You will be *seriously* impressed, and then most likely overwhelmed with feelings of inadequacy.) This woman does it *all*. Her husband has full confidence in her. She works with fabrics and is an entrepreneur. She is in the trading industry, invests in real estate, and even uses her earnings to buy a vineyard. (No big deal.) She watches over the affairs of her household, which in modern language means she monitors her children's online activity and not only knows their passcodes, but also the hidden apps they have on their phones. She is physically fit and goes about her work vigorously. She stays up way past dark and wakes up before dawn. She provides food for her family and is never lazy. She makes clothes and bedding for her household and extra garments to sell, even spinning her own thread! She is dressed in the finest clothes, and her beauty is more than skin-deep. She cares for the poor and needy. She speaks with wisdom and faithful instruction is on her tongue. Her children bless her. Her husband praises her.

Is she for real? Is this woman someone we could actually aspire to be? Can any one woman be and do all of these things? Before I tell you what most scholars believe about this perfect woman, let me show you what I believe is absolute proof that she is not an actual person—or at least that this description of her is not realistic or something we should use as a standard by which to measure ourselves. It's right there in the text, just half of a sentence, ". . . she can laugh at the days to come" (verse 25). There is no way this woman would be laughing at the days to come if she was drowning in the daily tasks of life. She would not be carefree or have much of a sense of humor if she was overworked, overwhelmed, sleep-deprived, making her food and clothing from scratch, pouring it out in her home and in her community day in and day out. No human being could sustain this kind of activity—not even a woman.

Time for a little context: this passage of Scripture is actually an acrostic poem, with each verse beginning with a successive letter of the Hebrew alphabet. Have you ever received a card where your child vertically spelled out your name and then used each letter to form words that describe their favorite things about you? That's what this is. It is a poem written to describe a noble woman.

Most scholars agree that rather than limiting a woman's role to any one area, this text presents the limitless opportunities and possible ways women can find fulfillment, both inside and outside their homes. Rather than creating unrealistic expectations and impossible standards for women to attain, this list actually *frees* women to live out their distinct callings and use their gifts. Thank God! I am free to look at this beautiful passage as an invitation to embrace how God created *me*. I can let go of unrealistic standards and expectations. I can explore and discover the unique ways God is leading me to find fulfillment, both inside and outside my home, honoring my Maker in all that I do.

You Be You

Many women do noble things, but you surpass them all.
—Proverbs 31:29

We all have certain skills and activities we think we are supposed to be good at and enjoy. If our mothers or grandmothers were great cooks, we may feel joy if we also love to cook. Or, we may feel a sense of failure that somehow that genetic trait skipped over us. I once complimented my friend, Marla, on the wonderful dinners she made for her family each night, and she immediately went into a full discourse about how much she did not enjoy cooking. "The whole food thing is such a hassle! I mean, you have to decide what to make, and then you have to go to the grocery store to get the ingredients. Then you have to do the prep work, cook the meal, and then listen to your kids complain that they don't like what you made for them. And then you have to clean up all the dishes! If there was a pill that would nutritionally sustain me and make me feel full, I would take it and give it to my family. I would just do away with the whole food thing all together."

For many years I tried to like gardening. I felt like I was supposed to be good at it and enjoy it. I had this expectation that good mothers taught their children how to garden. After all, it's spoken of all throughout the Bible—many of Jesus' stories have to do with planting seeds, yielding a harvest, vines and branches, and trees bearing fruit. Additionally, almost everyone I know does some kind of gardening, whether it's planting a few flowers in the spring or creating an elaborate vegetable garden (complete with composting) that produces a farm-to-table kind of lifestyle. My mom always had both flower and vegetable gardens, and she canned vegetables during the summer for us to enjoy during the winter. I can't say enough about my admiration for women like her. The dedication required to plant and maintain a garden is truly praiseworthy. And the miracle of what happens when you bury a seed, water it, and give it light—it's extraordinary.

Nevertheless, here is the truth about me: I do not like working in the hot sun. If I am going to be outside during the summer, I want to be sipping iced tea and talking with a friend or reading a good book—preferably in the shade. Also, I don't like to kneel or squat. Kneeling hurts my back and squatting makes me feel dizzy. Furthermore, I don't like dirt, and I especially don't like what happens to dirt when you add water to it. I also hate bugs and worms (typically found in dirt). Finally, I don't like that when you are finished gardening your flowers look beautiful, but then if you happen to forget to water them for a few days—or maybe water them too much—they shrivel up and die. I stopped planting flowers in our front yard years ago because I realized I was just setting myself up for humiliation with my neighbors. Inevitably, I would neglect to water the plants for days and then try to make up for my neglect by over-watering them. Within a few short weeks they would all be dead.

I have found great freedom in letting go of the pressure to enjoy gardening. I am perfectly happy buying my cucumbers and tomatoes at the grocery store. My friends know not to buy me plants, and there is something liberating about saying, "That's just really not my thing."

My friend, Tina, recalls a time when her daughter was in preschool, and it was her turn to bring in the snack for the day:

Some moms brought in elaborate homemade snacks, like rainbow fruit kabobs, freshly baked banana muffins, and apple sauce made from scratch. Other moms brought in less impressive but still homemade snacks, like actual "popped at home" popcorn or apple slices and peanut butter. And some of us moms brought in store bought snacks, like goldfish crackers, pretzels, and prepackaged apple sauce.

On this particular morning, after dropping my son, Tyler, off at kindergarten, Alyssa and I swung by the grocery store to pick up the snack for her to bring to class. We quickly chose a couple boxes of crackers—I don't even remember what kind—and made our way to the check-out lane. I do, however, remember how relieved I felt that I was able to get the snack and still make it to school on time, since I had forgotten to pick it up the day before. Whew! Mission accomplished, right?

As usual, when we arrived at school the children were excitedly greeting one another and parents and teachers were crowding around the door. I handed the snack to one of the teachers who looked inside the bag, smiled, and sweetly said, "Oh. You're the *simple* mom."

Ouch! That stung. And right in front of the other moms. I don't know if she intended to insult me, but it felt like a judgement. Her comment hit me at the core of my weakness. Creating elaborate food is not my specialty. Don't get me wrong—I love *eating* food, but for me, making it is just a necessary evil. When it was my turn to provide the snack, I didn't even entertain the idea of going through the trouble of creating an extraordinary food experience for the children. I looked at it as fulfilling my obligation. I got it done and I checked it off my list.

But you know what? Some moms thrive and find great joy in creating elaborate snacks for three-year-olds. More power to them! Making those snacks probably makes them feel really good. But for me, fulfilling my duty of providing a snack made *me* feel good. I kept it simple. I did what was required. I did it the way I do things best: simply and without complications.

I think sometimes we overcomplicate things by trying to achieve someone else's standards for what we should be doing. We try to be someone—aka Betty Crocker—that we are not. I don't want to spend my days worrying about what other people think of me and the way I do things. I just want to be me.

Which is why I decided to reframe that teacher's criticism into a personal acceptance statement. What she said is true. I *am* a simple mom, and it's not a negative thing. I don't try to be someone I am not. I can appreciate the unique ways other women are gifted and enjoy their elaborate creations, and at the same time be content with who I am—a woman who simply gets things done.

Outsourcing Parenting

I don't know what's more exhausting about parenting:
the getting up early, or the acting
like you know what you're doing.
—Jim Gaffigan

Is it bad parenting to offer to pay your older child ten
dollars to teach your younger child how to ride a two-
wheeler? At first, you might be tempted to judge me for being
a lazy parent.   You might ask, "Aren't moms and dads
supposed to teach their kids these things? What's next—
hiring a professional to potty train your toddler?" (There are
actually potty training consultants out there, and parents who
hire them.) In my defense, Bernie and I had successfully
taught both of our older daughters how to ride their two-
wheelers. The technique that worked for both of them was
removing the pedals from their bikes so they could
periodically touch their feet to the ground while they learned
how to balance. We tried the same technique with Brenna,
but it just did not work. She was weaving from side to side,
zigzagging down the sidewalk, continuously stopping and
starting.
    Until you've done it, you just cannot understand how *very
hard* it is on a mature person's back to run alongside a
balance-impaired child on a rickety bike, trying to keep her
upright by holding on to the back of her seat. This is much
easier for a young whippersnapper who is closer to the
ground and has less wear and tear on her joints. Besides,
what young person would not be motivated to earn an easy

ten bucks? I'll tell you who—both of my older daughters, who declined my generous offer. I finally found a taker when Kate's friend enthusiastically accepted the challenge. After a couple of hours with Sarah in the school parking lot, Brenna was ready to throw her training wheels away for good. It was the best ten dollars I had ever spent!

This concept of involving other people in the raising of our children is not a bad one. I tried to teach my older girls to play the piano, but getting them to practice and staying consistent with lessons was harder than I expected. I realized that hiring a piano teacher was a better way to go.

When Kate was contemplating quitting dance after eight years of lessons and recitals, I suggested she call her older cousin, Rachel, who had been a dancer for many years. The two of them talked it over, and Kate decided to take a semester off, then pick it up again later in the year. Now, many years later, Kate is in nursing school. On her hardest days, she texts Rachel to see if she is available. Kate knows that I am here for her whenever she wants to talk, but Rachel, who is also a nurse, can understand much better how Kate is feeling. She is better able to encourage Kate in exactly the way she needs. Rachel has had a consistent presence and influence in Kate's life, as well as with my other daughters.

When my pre-teen daughter, Brenna, was upset over a school-related situation, I listened and did my best to empathize, but then enlisted the help of her older sister, Claire. The girls talked late into the night—private conversations, the details of which I will never know. I went to bed that night content, knowing that by stepping back and allowing someone else to step in, my daughter received what she needed most—a friend who understood.

We cannot, on our own, give our kids everything they need. We won't always know the right approach or be able to offer the best advice. We won't always be able to understand what our child is experiencing. Sometimes, when we step out of the way and another trusted individual steps in, our children grow by leaps and bounds under the leadership of another. Even though it can be difficult at times to admit and accept my limitations as a parent, I am learning that I do not always have to be the one to give the lesson or have the life-changing conversation. It is healthy for my daughters to develop close bonds and be able to confide in safe people—it doesn't always have to be with me.

After my mom died, Brenna was having an especially hard time dealing with her loss. At eight years old, her grief was mixed with the fear that someone else she loved might die. She hadn't wanted to talk about my mom, she didn't like it when we mentioned her, and then one day, she asked if we could take Mom's picture down from our family room wall. It made her too sad to see it. During my mom's illness, I had given Brenna unlimited phone privileges with her grandma. Taking full advantage of this new freedom, Brenna called my mom frequently just to say hi, and to talk about whatever was happening that day. She grew closer to her grandma during those eight months than she had in all the years leading up to that point. After my mom's death I had tried repeatedly to talk with Brenna about her feelings and try to get her to open up, but she was pretty shut down. Finally, she shared how sad she felt because she didn't have a grandma anymore. It broke my heart. I felt helpless and didn't know what to do to support her.

One day, while eating her after-school snack, Brenna asked, "Mom, remember when Bunny took me after school to the grocery store and we bought cookie dough, and then we went back to her house, baked the cookies, and put together a puzzle?"

Bunny is a couple of years younger than my mom and has been my friend and mentor for nearly twenty years. When I was traveling back and forth to Michigan to be with my mom during her chemotherapy treatments, Bunny had offered to spend some time with Brenna and help Bernie with all he was juggling at home.

"Yes, I remember you telling me about your afternoon with Bunny." She had talked about it for days.

"Well, do you think we could do that again? Do you think I could spend time with Bunny again?"

I didn't know what my daughter needed, but she did. She needed time with Bunny. She was not trying to replace her grandma; she was ready to open up her heart and let others love her and help her through that very sad time.

I met Bunny for tea the following week and told her about my conversation with Brenna. She was deeply touched by Brenna's request and more than happy to fulfill it. When I told Brenna that Bunny was going to pick her up after school and take her on a date, she smiled and said, "I feel special."

Bunny took Brenna for frozen yogurt, and then they went to an animal supply store to pick up birdseed for Bunny's cockatiel, and even picked up a special toy for our dog, Lila. Afterwards, they bought carrots and stopped to feed some elk. Brenna came home beaming, and over dinner she talked about her time with Bunny. They hadn't talked about anything serious, just what they did that day, what Bunny does when she volunteers at our church's Care Center, and what Brenna does in school. She talked to Bunny like she used to do with my mom. It was perfect.

Over the years, friends, fellow parents, youth group leaders, aunts, uncles, cousins, and teachers have taught, mentored, and walked with our kids. As much as Bernie and I care about every aspect of our daughters' lives, we are not the only people they need. We are not always the best folks for the job. Pulling in trusted others who love our daughters and are good role models is an invaluable asset to our parenting.

As a mom, it is especially difficult for me to see my daughters go through hard seasons. I feel helpless when they are hurting, and I don't always know how to make it better. Encouraging my daughters to call a friend or a relative who may be able to relate or offer needed advice is something I am learning to do more often. This is not a competition. We all love these girls, and we are on the same team. Rather than feeling threatened or envious that someone else may be better able to meet a need and help my child in a specific situation, I've learned to ask for help, welcome the support, and be grateful I don't have to do this alone.

The "Me" in Mom

Make a careful exploration of who you are and the
work you have been given, and then sink yourself into
that. Don't be impressed with yourself. Don't compare
yourself with others. Each of you must take
responsibility for doing the creative best you can
with your own life.

—Galatians 6:4, THE MESSAGE

Several years ago, I attended my first writers' conference.
People sometimes ask me for advice about how to write and
publish a book, and I always tell them to go to a writers'
conference. It is the best way I know to hone your craft, learn
from professionals in the industry, meet other like-minded
aspiring writers, be inspired to write what is stirring within
you, and pitch your ideas to actual editors, publishers, and
agents. I showed up at that first conference with great
expectations, hoping to become a better writer and get my
articles published in magazines.

At the time, I had a monthly column in Chicago's *Daily
Herald* newspaper called, *A Mom's Point of View*. When you
introduce yourself to people you meet at a writers'
conference, you not only give your name and where you are
from; you also say what kind of writing you do. When I told
people that I wrote a newspaper column about motherhood,
I was given the same suggestion three times by three different
people. "You should speak at MOPS (Mothers of
Preschoolers) and moms' groups."

The first time someone offered this advice, I completely dismissed the idea. *No way, I don't want to be a speaker. I want to be a writer—that's why I'm here.* I was almost forty and had been a stay-at-home mom for twelve years. The stuttering problem I had developed when I was in elementary school was less frequent and severe than it had been in my teen and early adult years, but this was largely because I avoided stressful social situations and any event where I may be called on to speak publicly. As an adult, it's really not that hard to fly under the radar and just not do certain things. I was absolutely certain I did not want to be a speaker.

The second time someone suggested that I start speaking at MOPS, I was curious. As in, *That's interesting that you say that because just yesterday someone else said the exact same thing. But again . . . no.* On day three, I sat across from a young woman at lunch. She asked me what kind of writing I did and then literally interrupted me as soon as she heard me say the name of my column. "You should speak at MOPS! Actually, I'm a leader of a MOPS group here in Chicago, and you could speak at our group! Do you have a card?" I stared at her for a couple of seconds, my curiosity turning into a strange mix of anticipation and fear as I considered the possibility that perhaps God was calling me into something I never would have pursued on my own. I politely declined, explaining that I stuttered and how that disqualified me from speaking in front of groups. She wanted to hear more, and something about her sincerity and the questions she asked made it easy for me to open up.

I told her about the little girl I used to be—before I found out there was something wrong with me—and then about the anxiety, shame, and feelings of worthlessness that followed. We finished our lunch, and she asked if I wanted to walk around campus. When it started raining, we sat in her car and talked some more. I shared how, after years of struggling with anxiety and shame, I was finally beginning to find freedom as I opened myself up fully to God's love for me. It didn't bother him if I stuttered. It didn't diminish my value or make what I had to say any less significant. I was learning that even if people rejected me, God accepted me just as I was. His perfect love was strong enough to drive out my fears and insecurities. After years and years of practicing speech therapy and coping techniques, I had discovered that God's love sets me free.

I didn't understand why she was so interested in my story until she began to tell me hers. With tears streaming down her face, she told me about her own self-described defect—the thing about herself that she most wished she could change. She confessed the self-loathing she felt and how she had allowed this one thing to define her and fill her with shame. I'll never forget her humble request. Through her tears she said, "Becky, all of us have something we wish we could change, something for which we feel ashamed. So many women in my group also experience these feelings of worthlessness. They need the freedom and healing you have experienced. I want you to come share your story. Will you just come and share your story?"

Before we became moms, we were women with dreams, passions, gifts, and ideas. And before we became women, we were young girls with all of those same things. When I was a little girl, my favorite thing to play was pretend. I pretended to be a mother, practicing on my baby dolls and then on my baby sister when she came along. I pretended to be a cook, making mud pies and pizzas in the backyard, gathering stones and sticks to use for the "toppings." And I pretended to be a speaker of some kind: a teacher, a preacher, or a journalist. I used to record myself on my cassette-player/recorder using the attached microphone, imagining I was being interviewed for a Christian television program or radio show. I never thought much about this "play acting." I assumed every little girl did these same things.

Yet these were more than just childhood imagination and games—they were God-given dreams and desires he planted in my heart from a very young age. When I was playing with my dolls, the desire to mother a baby of my own someday was being birthed inside of me. Decades later, when I held each of my daughters for the first time, I remember feeling that I was *born* to be a mom. I'm not saying everything came naturally or that motherhood has been a piece of cake for me, but it is the most fulfilling thing I have done in my life.

Likewise, those pizza pies I made out of dirt and rocks—those were some of my earliest culinary creations. Turns out I am a total foodie—I work as a prep-chef, and when I'm at home you'll usually find me in the kitchen. Even after a full day of working at my job, I often enjoy unwinding in front of the stove, cooking dinner for my family.

My dream of becoming a speaker has been a bit more complicated—for many years I had forgotten it ever existed. Because of my speech difficulty, I was drawn to writing. It became the best way for me to express my thoughts and ideas, so as an adult it made sense for me to pursue writing opportunities. I fully intended to avoid public speaking of any kind for the rest of my life. Just give me a computer and a few hours alone, and I'll use my words to create something. Except that God made me a *communicator*, and writing was only part of that dream he placed within me from a young age. My desire to encourage others by weaving together stories and spiritual truths was not meant to be limited to the written word. God had given me a voice, and though for many years I hid it, he was about to uncover it. He wanted to use it. He wanted to show his power through my greatest weakness.

I said yes. I couldn't believe the words were coming out of my mouth, but I told this young woman I would come and speak to her group. I will never forget that first speaking engagement. The drive was about thirty minutes and all I could think was, *What am I doing? Why did I say yes to this?* I felt like I was going to throw up. When I arrived, one of the leaders welcomed me and offered to pray with me, which I gladly accepted. Several minutes later, as I approached the front of the room to begin my talk, my knees were shaking, and my mouth was dry. I had literally written out my story, and as I stood in front of that group of about twenty women, I read it to them, word for word. From time to time I looked up, making eye contact with a couple of the moms, and I could see that my story was resonating. Some of the moms had tears in their eyes, and they clapped when I finished. I felt like a child who had read a poem out loud in front of a room full of parents. I hadn't stuttered once, and even if I had, it wouldn't have mattered. I was free. I sat down at one of the tables where the women were going to discuss some questions related to what I had shared, and I felt a surge of joy and *something else.* I couldn't quite name it, but I heard God whisper—not audibly, but deep in my soul, "See, I knew you'd love it."

My children have watched me develop my gifts and commit myself to a process of growth. They have seen me face and overcome my fears, with God's help. They have cheered me on as I've said yes to opportunities to speak in front of groups and share my story. There is always something on my calendar that scares me, but with every yes I say, I find that God is faithful to give me the help I need to do what he has put before me. The release of my first book brought many new opportunities for me to speak and share my story, including several radio interviews. When I was in high school, my speech therapist had asked me to make a list of the scariest things I could ever imagine myself doing. Radio interviews were at the top of that list. As I prepared for my first interview, going over my notes and praying for God to help me and calm my nerves, I remembered that little girl with her microphone and tape recorder. I remembered that I was made for *this.*

My daughters have had a front row seat as I am becoming the woman I was created to be. We can't do it all. We weren't *made* to do it all. We don't need to try harder—we just need to try *better* to do what God, in his wisdom and perfect timing, has put in our hearts to do. Some women have a strong sense of who they are when they are young, but many women I know are discovering who they really are in their thirties, forties, and fifties. It's a discovering that never ends.

My friend, Julie, knew she wanted to be an artist from the time she was five years old. After graduation, she wanted to go to art school but was discouraged from pursuing art as a career in college. Her parents did not think it would be a successful option. Julie's interpretation of that message was that she would not be good enough to succeed as an artist, let alone explore other fields related to art. So she majored in Business—something "successful" in the eyes of the world, but the furthest thing from her heart's cry. Many years later, she began to fight for the calling on her life that she could not ignore. She took some art classes, built a photography business over the course of nine years, and then started her own ceramics studio. She has taken some risks and they have paid off. In her forties, she is now making her living as an artist. And the creative work God is doing in her life is even more stunning than the gorgeous pieces that come out of her shop.

For many of us, becoming mothers helps us remember who we were starting to become so many years ago. As we watch our children grow, it's like a door is opened and we get to slip through and grow with them. We remember the dreams God placed inside us, all those years ago. We get to open our hearts to new dreams he wants to deposit in our hearts in this current season. The more we can identify and shed the unrealistic and ill-fitting expectations we have picked up along the way, the more we are free to embrace and fan into flame the gifts that God planted in us from our youth. He heals and restores what was broken. He sets free that which was bound. He uncovers what has been hidden. He is making all things new. Moms, he isn't finished with us yet—he is faithful to complete the good work he started.

You be you. Be creative, funny, intellectual, simple, elaborate, soft-spoken or loud. Be introverted, extroverted, high-energy, low-key, enthusiastic, or chill. Wear make-up, or don't. Enjoy your cooking, gardening, or crafting. Go running, watch movies, or read novels. Teach, sing, write, or dance. Take care of patients, lead a bible study, run a corporation, or paint.

Whether we weave thread into fabric or words into stories, whether we are night owls or early risers, whether we make a hundred business deals or tacos for the hundredth Tuesday in a row, may we do it all to bring glory and honor to our God. May we reflect his love to the world around us. In the beautiful array of all our diversities, strengths, and talents, may we open our arms to the poor and extend our hands to the needy. May we speak with wisdom—may faithful instruction be on our tongues. May we be clothed with strength and dignity, free to laugh at the days to come. May our children arise and call us blessed, and our husbands give us praise.

"Charm is deceptive, and beauty is fleeting; but a woman who fears the Lord is to be praised" (verse 30).

Review:

No matter how hard we try, we cannot have it all, do it all, and be everything to all people at all times. When we understand and embrace the way God has created each of us, we can let go of unrealistic standards and expectations. We remember some of the dreams he placed in us from our youth. We can explore and discover the unique ways God is leading us to find fulfillment, both inside and outside our homes, honoring our Maker in all that we do.

Reflect:

1. What is something you think you are supposed to enjoy or be good at, but it's just not your thing—no matter how hard you try? How would it feel to acknowledge and accept it, and then celebrate those things that truly make your heart sing?

2. Do your children have other reliable individuals besides you (and your spouse) in their lives? If not, how can you begin to create a support team, pulling in trusted others who will be godly mentors and influencers?

3. What level of fulfillment are you currently experiencing, both inside and outside your home? Are there any dreams from your youth that God may be stirring up, wanting to revive?

Respond:

God, thank you for making me the way that I am. "For you created my inmost being; you knit me together in my mother's womb. I praise you because I am fearfully and wonderfully made; your works are wonderful, I know that full well" (Psalm 139:13-14). Help me to let go of unrealistic expectations, people-pleasing, comparison, and the need to impress others. Give me a clear sense of what you have set before me and help me to work at it with all my might. Free me to be content with who I am. Help me to find fulfillment in doing my creative best with the life you have given me. Amen.

#11—The Most Important Thing Is That Your Kids Be Happy

Always Follow Your Heart

The heart is deceitful above all things and beyond cure.
Who can understand it?
—Jeremiah 17:9

Behind the advice "always follow your heart" is the idea that our hearts will always lead us well and never steer us off track. But sometimes, attempting to follow our hearts is like being dropped off in the middle of a remote, unfamiliar place on a cloudy day without a compass and then trying to find our way back home. *Hmmm…I really feel like maybe home is west of where I am right now. And if I can trust my gut, it's telling me north is that way* … Or, we may know the direction we are supposed to move towards, but we can't resist the pull to follow the crowd and be like everyone around us. Jeremiah was known as the "weeping prophet" as he delivered God's rebuke and warning to the people of Israel. Their hearts had strayed and turned away from the Lord, and in their rebellion they were headed towards oppression, slavery, and destruction. His observation, "The heart is deceitful above all things and beyond cure. Who can understand it?" follows several chapters of him pleading for God's people to return to their Maker.

Our desires and emotions are powerful and have tremendous sway over us, but they are often unreliable. Like trying to navigate our way home without a compass or a map, following our hearts can get us lost in the worst way. "The heart wants what the heart wants" may be true, but sometimes what our hearts want is in opposition to what God wants. Sometimes what our hearts want will not provide lasting peace and joy. Too often, our hearts are focused on our immediate cravings for happiness and pleasure, our intense needs for security and approval, or our desire to avoid discomfort at all costs. Our hearts are not always seeking to do what is wise and right. Our hearts are not always concerned with the long-term consequences of our actions.

We've already talked about the problematic advice "always trust your motherly instincts." When we are driven by fear, guilt, insecurities, and our needs for acceptance and approval, our perspective is often skewed. Our maternal instincts can prove to be very untrustworthy.

Yet in parenting, there is another aspect of "following our hearts" that can have such disastrous consequences that it warrants an entirely separate chapter. This pitfall may be more subtle and harder to identify. On the surface, it can even appear to be selfless and loving. We hear it all the time, and it has become a mark of good parenting: "All I want is for my kids to be happy." You may be asking, "What is wrong with wanting my kids to be happy? Doesn't every parent want that?" Yes. Every good parent wants their children to be happy. But when our primary desire is for our children to be happy and for life to be easy for them, and when their happiness is derived from temporary satisfaction, we can find ourselves parenting from a short-sighted perspective. If all I want is for my kids to be happy, I will panic at every sign of struggle. I will look for shortcuts. I will intervene and try to "fix" every problem. And if I make the terrible mistake of making my children's happiness my number one priority, doing everything in my power to make them happy and keep them happy, I will be in danger of raising children who feel entitled, take the easy way out instead of the best way forward, give up when the going gets tough, and depend on others to make them happy. They will seek the next thing that will bring them pleasure and choose personal comfort over obedience to God.

God is our perfect Father, and he doesn't parent us with the goal of making and keeping us happy. He is always loving us, providing for us, caring for us, and shaping our character. But he does not always spare us discomfort and pain, coddle us so we never experience hardship, and remove our troubles at the first sign of distress. At least that has not been my experience, and it is not what Scripture teaches. Contemplate this perspective in James 1:2-4: "Consider it pure joy, my brothers and sisters, whenever you face trials of many kinds, because you know that the testing of your faith produces perseverance. Let perseverance finish its work so that you may be mature and complete, not lacking anything."

James writes to us as a brother, encouraging us to let God do his work so we may grow up and be mature and complete. I don't know about you, but my heart will choose the easy path *every time*. My heart will seek to avoid pain and discomfort at all costs. My heart will tell me to run the other way when I see trials up ahead. Our wise, loving Father is not interested in raising spoiled, sheltered, self-centered children, and we shouldn't be either. Rather, he is shaping us into children who love him and love others, who are willing to sacrifice to do what is right, who persevere through trials, and look to him as their source of joy and strength. He is raising his kids to seek his kingdom more than pleasure, and obedience more than comfort.

As painful as it may be, the truth is that sometimes our children need to feel miserable because they have made poor choices. Sometimes they need to feel disappointed to discover that God is the only one who will never let them down. Sometimes they need to fail so they can find their identity and worth in Christ. Sometimes they need to go without so they can learn to appreciate their abundance of blessings. Sometimes they need to struggle so they can grow. They need to cry so they can be comforted and hurt so they can be healed.

As parents, sometimes we need to get out of God's way. We need to *not* step in and try to "fix it." Our efforts to rescue, protect, and make things better can actually short-circuit the work he is trying to do in his children's lives. It is one thing to believe that God works in and through our many trials, strengthening our faith and developing perseverance in our lives. Yet, an even deeper level of faith is required when we entrust our children to this process, "letting perseverance finish its work so that they may be mature and complete, not lacking anything" (James 1:4).

The Yellow Mug

It's a bittersweet road we parents travel. We start with
total commitment to a small, helpless human being.
Over the years we worry, plan, comfort,
and try to understand.
We give our love, our labor, our knowledge, and our
experience—so that one day he or she will have the
inner strength and confidence to leave us.
—Adele Faber

Our eldest daughter, Kate, called me at work. She was
crying. She had just hung up the phone with the admissions
officer from the college she was hoping to attend in the fall.
This small, private school was out of our price range, but she
had been invited to apply and interview for a merit-based full
scholarship. A few weeks earlier, she and I had spent the
weekend visiting the college, touring the campus, meeting
with several of the faculty, and getting an in-depth look at
their stellar nursing program. As we strolled through the brick
paved streets of this cute little college town, Kate and I both
began to imagine what her college experience there might
be like. A full scholarship would be amazing. We could use
the money we had saved for her education to buy her a car,
giving her independence and freedom. She already had a
lead on a part-time job in the admissions office, and since
she would only be about three hours away, she could come
home on the weekends whenever she wanted. Maybe this
was the way God was going to provide for her. Our hopes

were high. Kate was not nearly as confident as Bernie and I—we thought for sure she would make it. Of course we did! We are her parents and we know how extraordinary she is. The wait had been hard, but finally, she got the call.

"Mom, I didn't get it," she said through her tears. Only eight of the one hundred applicants were chosen, and Kate did not make the cut. The admissions counselor told her it had been a very difficult decision and the competition had been fierce. He hoped, of course, she would still enroll in the fall and reminded her she would still receive the highest academic scholarship they offered, short of the full ride. But the reality was that without that scholarship she would not be able to attend the school. Even with the partial scholarship and grants, the tuition was more than we could afford, and we felt that the student loans would be too burdensome.

We had been praying for God to open or close the door, according to His plan. But now that the door had been closed, Kate did what many of us do. She turned inward. She blamed herself. She wondered what she had done wrong. She asked the same question I've asked when I've faced rejection and disappointment. *Why wasn't I good enough?*

It is painful for me to see my children hurting. I want my children to be happy, and when a problem arises that causes pain or discomfort, I have this overwhelming desire to "fix it." I want to fast-forward through the process and short-circuit the pain. I long to make the hurt go away.

When I got home from work that afternoon, I went into full fix-it mode. I told Kate's younger sisters that she didn't get the scholarship. "Don't say anything to her or ask her any questions. She needs space—just leave her alone."

I texted my sister, Kari, and my friend, Margie, and told them she didn't get it. I asked them to pray for her. I walked into the kitchen where my husband was washing dishes, and I saw the yellow mug on the counter. Kate had purchased it from a cute little coffee shop the weekend we visited the college for her interview. Everything about that cup represented the hope that she would end up in that quaint little town, in the nursing program at the school that had become her first choice.

"Bernie—quick—wash that mug and I'll put it away in the cabinet, behind the other mugs. She'll be upset if she sees it. It will just remind her of what happened." It was a knee-jerk reaction, and later, when I told Margie about me scrambling to hide the mug, I was surprised she questioned me about it.

Margie knows me well. We've been friends for a really long time. She knows my story and understands my tendency to try to control things. And, she has a habit of asking probing, character-revealing questions at precisely the right moment.

"Becky, why did you move the mug?"

At the time, it seemed like a caring, sensitive gesture. I was trying to spare my daughter even more pain. But as I began to explain my reasons to Margie, it became increasingly clear that my actions were more about me than my daughter, more about managing my own discomfort in seeing her disappointed than truly helping and supporting her through the heartbreak. Instead of honoring and respecting the process, I was driving the getaway car, yelling to her through the passenger window, "Get in! I know a shortcut—I'll get you out of here in a jiffy!"

It wasn't the first time I had tried to minimize pain in my children's lives. When they were infants, our pediatrician recommended we give them "tummy time" to help strengthen and develop their abdominal muscles. All of my daughters hated it and would cry after only a few seconds, so I'd flip them over on their backs where they were more comfortable. I couldn't stand to see them struggle. I hated to hear them cry. I wanted giggles and smiles, and I did not have the vision I needed to appreciate how the struggle would make them stronger, how they would grow through the tears.

As the girls grew and explored new interests and friendships, it broke my heart each time they didn't make a team or were slighted by a friend. At times, I had to suppress my desire to call a teacher, coach, choir director, or fellow parent to advocate on behalf of my child or challenge a decision that I thought was unfair or unkind.

In addition, over the years I had often been quick to hand out consequences for disrespectful attitudes or disobedience, only to later revoke them because some special circumstance made the punishment too painful or inconvenient. I'd tell myself I was giving grace, when really I was just giving in, catering to my own discomfort rather than following through on the hard stuff in order to build character.

Kate waited several days before telling anyone about her closed door, but I did not, and this caused a problem between us. I explained my motivation for telling her sisters, Kari, and Margie, and she firmly told me it was her news to share—that I should have waited and let her tell them when she was ready. I tried to explain that I was just trying to help and protect her—that I didn't want them to say something that would upset her even more—and then she asked me a question that stopped me in my tracks.

"Do you really think so little of me that you didn't think I could handle this? What were you afraid I would do? Were you afraid I wouldn't be able to get through it?"

In that moment, it became painfully clear to me that instead of sparing my daughter additional pain, I had added to it. I had been so sure she would be awarded the scholarship, but I had not communicated my confidence in her ability to handle the outcome, whatever that turned out to be.

There are, of course, no short-cuts. The only way through is through. And most often, pain is the pathway to growth. Good parenting requires an understanding of the value of the growth process, and a conviction that in our difficult circumstances God is doing his creative work, shaping and forming our children into who he created them to be. He is always working to transform us into people who resemble his Son. Suffering and disappointment are some of his most useful tools.

Kate did get through it. She grew through it. She developed some muscles and resilience that will serve her well in life. The following fall she began her studies at a fantastic school where God opened wide the door, a school with a superb nursing program within our price range. And, with a little time and perspective, she began to see that this school was a great fit for her. She began to feel a sense of belonging.

Shortly before my mom died, during one of our last conversations in the hospital as I sat by her bedside, she went over some last-minute details with me: some things about her apartment and final arrangements she had made, some paperwork, and loose ends. Then, she looked at me and said with all the confidence in the world, "Becky, you are going to be OK."

She couldn't protect me from what was about to happen. She couldn't minimize the loss and pain I would feel after she was gone. But in that moment, she was telling me she believed in me. She believed that with God's help, I would get through it. I would be able to handle the outcome, whatever that turned out to be.

God's top priority is not for us to be happy. He doesn't always spare us from pain and discomfort, but he does promise to be with us and help us in all our troubles. He draws us near and parents us in all the right ways. Sometimes, what our children need most is time and space to grow. They need to know we are here for them and we believe in them. Sometimes they need us to leave the yellow mug on the counter, so it can be transformed into an opportunity for them to experience the ever-present help and faithfulness of God.

It's Not Fair!

Fair doesn't mean giving every child the same thing, it
means giving every child what they need.
—Rick Lavoie

It is perhaps the most classic complaint kids throw at their
parents—classic because it's the complaint we used to throw
at our parents when we were growing up. "It's not fair!"
When the younger sister gets her ears pierced at the age of
nine and the older sister got hers done at twelve, the older
sister cries, "It's not fair!" When all the other kids in sixth
grade have cell phones and you tell your daughter she can't
have one until eighth grade, she protests, "It's not fair!" When
the older child (who has a job and drives her parents' car) is
expected to pay for some of her own expenses while the
younger child is completely dependent on her parents for all
things financial, the older child calls foul and argues, "It's not
fair!" Though we are quick to reply (as did our parents),
"Well, life's not fair!" we may, if we are honest, see areas in
our own lives where this root of envy rears its ugly head.

The neighbors are upgrading their automobiles and
renovating their house—again—while we can't seem to keep
up with household repairs and expenses. *It's not fair!* Friends
on Facebook post photos from their recent vacations to
tropical paradises and we wonder how on earth they can
afford to fly their entire family to Hawaii for two weeks? *It's
not fair!* Your best friend's daughter is easy-going and obedient,
and "strong-willed" doesn't even begin to describe your son
and the battles that ensue as a result of his hard-wired

inflexibility. *It's not fair.* Most people you know lead healthy, normal lives while you or your loved one suffers with a chronic illness. *It's so not fair.* The couples at church seem to be happy and satisfied, and we wonder if we are the only ones who are struggling in our marriage? *It's not fair.* When we focus our attention on what we have compared to what someone else has, we become ensnared in a trap. Comparison has a way of breeding discontentment, and it can be a difficult cycle to break.

Envy can be defined as resenting God's goodness in someone else's life while failing to recognize it in our own. Numerous times throughout the years, our children have told Bernie and me about all the ways we have not been fair. We are sometimes accused of "playing favorites." It's as if each child has a unique filter through which they interpret our decisions, and in an effort to change and correct those filters, I try to explain and defend why we have made the choices we have made. And yet, before I can begin to help my children identify envy and eradicate it from their lives, I have to take an honest look at my own heart. I need to understand my own filters and perceptions and recognize where envy has taken root.

Part of the problem is the way we choose to make sense of our lives and equate fairness with justice. Some of the things that happen to us are completely outside of our control. Other things happen to us as consequences because of choices we make. And things happen to other people that have absolutely nothing to do with us. But we use all of it to try to make sense of who God is and the way he works and how he shows his love. In his book, *New Morning Mercies*, Paul David Tripp writes that God

takes the disasters in your life and makes them tools of redemption. He takes your failure and employs it as a tool of grace. He uses the 'death' of the fallen world to motivate you to reach out for life. The hardest things in your life become the sweetest tools of grace in his wise and loving hands. So be careful how you make sense of your life. What looks like a disaster may in fact be grace. What looks like the end may be the beginning. What looks hopeless may be God's instrument to give you real and lasting hope. Your Father is committed to taking what seems so bad and turning it into something that is very, very good.[9]

While Bernie and I do not intentionally favor one child over another or act unjustly in what we give, our highest priority is *not* to try to make our children happy by being fair and making everything equal in their eyes. God is our perfect parent and he doesn't parent us this way. His highest priorities are not to make us happy, to do what we think is fair, and to make everything equal in our eyes. He has no internal need to please us or keep us happy in order to feel good about himself. He always does what is right and never feels guilty, even when we misunderstand him, jump to inaccurate conclusions, or judge his intentions as anything other than loving. He gives us what we need when we need it. He works all things for our good. He loves us in the way we most need to be loved. He allows us to experience weakness and lack and discomfort *so that* he can show his power, his provision, and his comfort. Why do we think that everything should be fair and equal and the same, when God is writing a unique story in each one of our lives?

If we are to parent our children the way God parents us, then our goal will be to do the right thing at the right time, to do what makes sense for our family (even if it's not what made sense a few years ago), and to help our children develop a perspective that recognizes God's goodness in their own lives and celebrates it in the lives of others. But contentment must begin with me. My friend's mother used to say that if we all collectively dumped our life's unwanted stuff in a pile and could pick up whatever we wanted, we'd each probably take back our own stuff. I can look at the person on my left and begrudge that he or she is experiencing greater wealth, health, or happiness than I am. But then I look at the person on my right and see that he or she is dealing with issues far more difficult than mine. It would do me well to reflect on God's activity in my own life and stop comparing what I have or don't have to those around me. Because when I think about God's faithfulness and provision, when I think about how he has never once left me alone or without hope, when I think about how he has made a way for me through my darkest valleys, how could I ever say he has been anything other than good?

Backwards Prayers

It didn't take me long to realize that I did my best
parenting by prayer. I began to speak less to the kids
and more to God. It was actually quite relaxing.

—Paul E. Miller

I said I'd never do it again. After having the worst garage
sale in the history of garage sales several years ago, I decided
that it was too much work and not worth the reward. (When
I subtracted what I spent on garage sale signs, I made forty
dollars. And I still had to get rid of all my junk.) But
apparently for me, garage sales are similar to childbirth,
because two years later I changed my mind.

Let's try this again. This time will be different. I dug my garage sale
signs out of our basement, which only added to my optimism.
*See, now I'll get my money's worth out of these signs by reusing them. Anything
I make today is pure profit. This time is going to be a success. We've got more
stuff. We've got better stuff.*

We had a kitchen table and chairs, a twin bed, and a
million smaller items that I was convinced would be sure
treasure for some lucky bargain hunters. Our friends dropped
off a piece of furniture and a framed map of the world which
sold in the first half hour. The sales were few and far
between, and by mid-morning, my garage sale fail really
began to do a number on me. I mean, what kind of world
are we living in when you put all your tasteful junk in your
driveway and people won't even pay good money for it?

And it wasn't just rejection that I felt. I felt a sense of
failure because I had made this garage sale into something

much bigger than an outdoor purging event. You see, during the summer, I work fewer hours. I enjoy the extra time at home with my kids, but my pay checks are smaller. And our bills are bigger: school registrations, property taxes due the beginning of August, driver's education, summer camps, and a family reunion in northern Michigan. And did I mention my daughter, Brenna, had gotten braces just in time to start middle school? Thousands of dollars of crisscrossed wire, putting pressure on her teeth and on our bank account. So I decided I'd do something smart and productive, and show my kids that hard work and determination really do pay off. I'd clean out our house and make a few bucks in the process.

The first part of the morning was fun. Bernie, Brenna, and I sat at our kitchen table at the end of our driveway and played Uno. Then we had breakfast. As I said a quick prayer of thanks for my toast and coffee, I slipped in a request for God to bless our garage sale and that we would sell lots of our stuff. After "Amen," I looked around and muttered, "I sure hope I sell most of it."

That's when Brenna casually challenged me. "Mom, maybe you should try praying backwards." I was intrigued. "Praying backwards? What does that mean? And where did you hear about it?"

"I read about it in the book I got at youth camp. Praying backwards is when, instead of asking God for what you want, you stop first and think about what Jesus wants. And you pray for that first."

I stared at my daughter in stunned silence. What would Jesus want? It occurred to me that he might not care all that much if I sold my bed or table, my lamps or tea kettle. He would be much more interested in the *people* coming to my house. He'd be looking for opportunities to interact with, love, and bless them. And, because Jesus had a history of engaging with all sorts of people and a gift for seeing past the exterior into the heart, I think Jesus would be interested in what was going on in *my* heart. He'd want to talk about my anxieties and my tendency to try to control outcomes.

My garage sale was a ridiculous flop, and I was super frustrated and exhausted after hauling stuff back down to our basement and to the trunk of our minivan. When I finally collapsed into bed that night, I could not stop thinking about the backwards prayers.

I've been a Christian for a really long time. But Brenna's words about how we approach prayer challenged me. The next day, I went into her bedroom before bed and asked her to tell me more about what she was reading. The book she got at youth camp is called *The Essential Guide to My New Life with Jesus*, by Scott Rubin, a long-time friend of ours and Brenna's junior high youth pastor at that time.[10] Brenna doesn't love to read, but she could hardly put this book down. It hooked her. So, when she finished it, I borrowed the book and learned how to pray backwards. It takes some getting used to. I began to see that often times, my first instinctual prayer is about my own comfort or the comfort of those I love. It's not that it's bad to pray for these things—it's certainly not wrong to ask God to bless my efforts and hard work at my garage sale, or in any other area of my life. But praying backwards invites us into something broader, deeper, and better. It requires us to look at what might be even more important than our immediate felt needs or wants. It reminds us that often times our prayers are small and limited—that God is able to do far above and beyond what we could even think or ask, more than we could ever imagine.

As my daughter and I have talked about and practiced praying this way, we've seen some pretty cool things happen. I had been praying for a close friend of mine who had been treated unfairly and deeply wounded by a friend. I prayed for healing for her, and I imagined myself secretly confronting this person who caused such deep feelings of rejection and emotional pain. And then, when I asked myself, "What would Jesus want?" I wondered if my friend had forgiven this person. I was pretty sure Jesus would want my friend's heart to be free from bitterness and unforgiveness, so I prayed along those lines. A few days later I was stunned when my friend (who didn't know I had been praying for her and this situation) told me that not only had she reached out to this person who had treated her so badly and offered to help her with a huge project, but she actually felt okay about it. While the relationship was not restored and the friendship didn't return to the way it used to be, I saw tremendous growth in my friend. I watched as her heart was set free from resentment. I watched her forgive.

When praying for a family friend (and family members) battling cancer, Brenna prayed, "God, I pray that you would help them and that their hearts would be open to you." As a mom, my prayers for my daughters are changing as I think first about what Jesus wants. My requests shift from "let my child be happy, let things go well for her . . ." to "use whatever you choose— disappointments, challenges, even my own shortcomings as a parent—to bring my child closer to you." These are big-picture prayers.

I will always pray for protection and help and for things to go well for my daughters, because I am a mom and that is what I desire. But as I pray backwards, I am discovering the short-sightedness in having this be my default prayer or the only prayer I pray on behalf of my children. I do want my kids to be happy, but that is not *all* I want. I want them to be rooted and grounded in God's love (Ephesians 3:17-19), to find their identity and worth in him when they battle insecurities (1 John 3:1), and to grow and mature as they navigate their way through all sorts of changes, disappointments, and struggles (James 1:4). I am praying that in the midst of their anxieties they learn to trust God from the bottom of their hearts (Proverbs 3:5, THE MESSAGE), and that his perfect love drives out every one of their fears (1 John 4:18). I'm praying they shine brightly like stars in the universe as they hold firmly to the word of life (Philippians 2:15-16), and that they love others well (1 Peter 1:22). I'm praying they grow closer to Jesus each day and are filled with true joy that doesn't depend on what is happening around them (Romans 15:13). I pray they will discover his strength in their weaknesses (2 Corinthians 12:9), and that his plans for them are for good and not for evil, to give them a future and a hope (Jeremiah 29:11).

Our family friend, the one battling cancer, says that these days she is feeling grateful more than anything else. Because God is using her current trials to open her eyes to all the good in her life, and she appreciates her time with her loved ones more than ever before. She is doing her best to let God lead her life every day.

I am also thankful for what I'm learning from my daughters, my friends, and our junior high youth pastor. I'm grateful for the reminder that God's plans and desires for us are better than we could even ask or imagine.

"Now to Him who is able to do immeasurably more than all we ask or imagine, according to His power that is at work within us, to Him be glory . . . Amen" (Ephesians 3:20-21).

Review:

If all I want is for my kids to be happy, I will panic at every sign of struggle. I will look for shortcuts. I will intervene and try to "fix" every problem. And I will be in danger of raising children who feel entitled, take the easy way out instead of the best way forward, give up when the going gets tough, and depend on others to make them happy. They will seek the next thing that will bring them pleasure and choose personal comfort over obedience to God.

We have a perfect Father, and he doesn't parent us with the goal of making and keeping us happy. He does not always spare us discomfort and pain, coddle us so we never experience hardship, and remove our troubles at the first sign of distress. He is, however, always loving us, providing for us, caring for us, and shaping our character.

Reflect:

1. How do you respond when your children are struggling or hurting? Can you relate to Becky's tendency to try to rescue them from hardships, fix their problems, or protect them from pain at any cost?

2. Are there areas in your own life where envy has taken root? How can you cultivate contentment and help your children develop a perspective that recognizes God's goodness in their own lives and celebrates it in the lives of others?

3. What do you think about the idea of "backwards prayers?" In addition to praying for everyday situations and immediate answers to prayer, what "big-picture" prayers can you begin to lift up to God as you think about

what he might want to do in your child's life? (The following prayer can give you some guidance . . .)

Respond:

God, thank you that you are our perfect Father. I pray that my children will be rooted and grounded in your love (Ephesians 3:17-19), will find their identity and worth in you when they battle insecurities (1 John 3:1), and will grow and mature as they navigate their way through all sorts of changes, disappointments, and struggles (James 1:4). I pray that in the midst of anxieties they learn to trust you from the bottom of their hearts (Proverbs 3:5, THE MESSAGE), and that your perfect love will drive out every one of their fears (1 John 4:18). I pray they shine brightly like stars in the universe as they hold firmly to the word of life (Philippians 2:15-16), and that they love others well (1 Peter 1:22). I pray they grow closer to you, Jesus, each day and are filled with true joy that doesn't depend on their circumstances (Romans 15:13). I pray they will discover your strength in every one of their weaknesses (2 Corinthians 12:9), and I thank you that your plans for them are for good and not for evil, to give them a future and a hope (Jeremiah 29:11). Amen.

#12—You Are in Control

The Dance of Motherhood

To describe my mother would be to write about a hurricane in its perfect power. Or the climbing, falling colors of a rainbow.

—Maya Angelou

From the moment we become mothers, our instinct to hold on tightly to our child is powerfully present. And I'm not just talking about the moment we hold our child for the first time: it begins earlier than that. Whether we biologically carry and give birth to our children or become mothers through adoption, our maternal grip is fierce. We feel the baby move inside us—or feel our hearts move towards the child another woman has carried—and we actively wait for and pray for and do all we can to protect this little life that God is entrusting into our care.

When we hold our newborns, we do it ever-so-carefully, reminding anyone who comes within two feet of the child, "Be careful with her head! Make sure to support her neck!" We keep one hand on the baby's tummy while reaching for the baby wipes so he doesn't roll off the changing table. We strategically place mirrors in our cars so we can see our baby's face at all times. We wake up our sleeping baby just to make sure she is breathing,

And then, almost immediately, we are required to begin letting go. Our baby learns how to roll over—away from us. Our active crawler begins pulling up on furniture and soon we are hunched over, our child's tiny fingers curled around ours as we walk with our little one gleefully dancing beneath us. Then, when we think they can make it a few steps on their own, we let go. We let go and watch them toddle—even fall—as they take their first steps in this world. Before we know it, we are running behind them as they pedal their bikes, holding on to the seat until we sense they may be able to do it on their own, and we let go. We watch as they wobble down the sidewalk; we cheer like crazy whether they wipe out or make it to the end of the street, and if they do manage to keep their balance and the wheels turning, our elation turns to panic as we run behind them, yelling, "Stop! Stop at the end of the sidewalk! Watch for cars!"

They are growing up just like they are supposed to, but a part of our hearts cry, *Don't go too far! Please. Don't grow up too fast.* We celebrate their accomplishments and we burst with pride at every milestone realized: sports victories and dance recitals, academic achievements and eighth grade graduation. We drop them off for their first day of work. We watch them back the car out of the driveway for their first solo ride and we breathe a prayer of protection. Before we know it, we are standing with other incredulous parents and taking a million photos as our beautiful daughters and handsome sons pose for homecoming, prom, and high school graduation pictures. As moms, we live with the constant tension of wanting to hold on yet needing to let go. This is the dance of motherhood. It is a tug-of-war between our desire to control and the reality that we cannot.

When children are young, they believe that their mothers have absolute control over the universe and consequently, as they get older, they blame their mothers for all sorts of things. It is two sides of the same coin. It rains on the day you were supposed to go to the pool and your child blames you. He falls while running on the sidewalk, scraping up his knee, and through hot tears screams, "You made me fall!" Your preteen daughter is having a bad hair day, and it's because you bought the wrong mousse. Your daughter is angry because she can't get her driver's license on her actual birthday because she didn't get her driving hours completed, and it's your fault. The spaghetti sauce tastes "different" and your kids want to know what you did to it, even though it's the same jarred marinara you've been buying since before they were born.

A friend of mine likes to tell how she got her teenaged daughter to stop blaming her for everything. She said, "You can keep blaming me for everything that goes wrong in your life as long as you give me credit for everything that goes right." Her daughter got the message. Yet as much as we detest being blamed for everything under the sun, we often perpetuate this blame game by trying to control everything and everyone around us. Within moments of our children being born we realize just how little control we really have, but that doesn't stop us from trying.

One day I was talking to my sister, Kari, and I heard her tell one of her older children to give her daughter, Maggie, the remote control with no batteries. The older kids were playing Wii, and one-year-old Maggie wanted to play too. The visual of my nephew giving Maggie a remote control with no batteries so she could point it at the TV, push buttons, and think she was playing video games with her siblings made me laugh. What a perfect example of the illusion of control.

Our remote controls don't have any batteries. Turns out, we do not run the universe. We cannot simultaneously take all the heat *and* all of the credit for how things turn out. This is where our faith comes in. As much as we are able, we entrust our children to God who gave them to us in the first place. It doesn't mean we won't still aim our remotes and push the buttons, because we will. But we remember that

God is trustworthy. He understands this desire we have to try to make everything turn out OK, so he gently reminds us over and over again that we can trust him with it all.

Stubborn for God

It's not easy raising strong-willed children, but what a
blessing it will be to watch that same child grow into an
uncompromising, unshakeable, determined adult.

—Amy Weatherly

Most of us don't view stubbornness as a desirable trait.
We feel exasperated when our children (or our spouses)
demonstrate this dogged determination—this unwillingness
to change their attitude or position on something—even
when given good reason to do so. We complain about our
strong-willed children who make our lives difficult. I
remember telling my Mom how stubborn my young
daughters were, and she graciously reminded me that I was
also strong-willed—in fact, the strongest-willed of her five
children—and she didn't view it as a bad thing. She said this
trait, though challenging, can be very positive when
harnessed for good. It had certainly been taxing on her when
I was little, but the upside was that as I got older, I was not
easily swayed. Sometimes that meant I stubbornly resisted
different ideas and wasn't always open to new opportunities,
like when the girls' basketball coach tried to get me to play
basketball in middle school. (At eleven years old I was 5'8".)
He was relentless in his pursuit, but I was more so in my
rejection. I didn't want to do it. The image of me dribbling a
basketball down the court with all eyes on me was terrifying.
The competitive nature of sports and the need to perform
well under pressure scared me. I never even considered
trying out. Other times, my strong will protected me from

making bad choices. A friend in high school repeatedly tried to get me to smoke cigarettes, but I had decided I wasn't ever even going to try them. I never even entertained the possibility of giving into her peer pressure because I had made up my mind. I stubbornly persisted in my refusal.

Truth is, I am still pretty stubborn. I have found this to be an asset in parenting strong-willed children, because in my hardest moments I only have to be a little more stubborn than my child. I only need to be a tad more tenacious than her as I hold the line. When I am parenting with wisdom and maturity, my stubbornness serves me well. But too often, I am aware that my stubborn attitude is really more about me and my desire to have things a certain way.

For several years when my children were younger, I met weekly with a friend to pray for our kids. One week my friend said an unusual prayer—one that I had never heard before. She prayed that her kids would be stubborn for God, and that they would follow after Him in a determined, persistent way. Her pastor had recently preached a sermon on what it means to be "stubborn for God" and that phrase stuck in my mind. For days, I thought about what this might look like—not stubborn to get my own way or hold on to my own point of view, but stubborn for God's ways and his will. I admit there are still many times I am stubborn for myself—stubborn because I want my way and I want to be right. To be stubborn for God means laying down my own agenda and desires in any situation and being determined to do what he wants instead. Jesus was stubborn for His Father in the way He lived and the way He loved others. His heart was set to do his Father's will, even when it battled against his own. He spoke out against injustice and meaningless religiosity. He loved the unlovable. He was determined to persistently go after those who were lost and hurting. He was stubborn all the way to the Cross, not stubborn for himself but stubborn for God and His plan. He was stubborn for *us*. The result of his stubbornness was that death could not overcome Him. The grave could not hold Him. Jesus Christ was perhaps the most stubborn person who ever lived—stubborn to save, stubborn to love, stubborn to live again and give us life eternal.

I pray that God would take my stubbornness—even in the way I parent—and use it to make me stubborn for *him* and the things that matter to his heart. I pray that our children would be stubborn for God, and that no matter how the world may try to persuade them to wander and go their own way they would hold fast to the truth. I continue to pray that, being firmly rooted in God's love, they would be difficult to move—stubborn for him in every way.

No Formulas

*In his hand is the life of every creature
and the breath of all mankind.*
—Job 12:10

"Train up a child in the way he should go: and when he is old, he will not depart from it" (Prov 22:6, King James Version). This verse has long been a favorite among parents. It encourages those of us with younger children to be diligent in raising them up in the ways of the Lord. And for those with older children who may be wandering off the faith path we started them on, this proverb provides hope and assurance that they will return. We hold on to these words when we feel discouraged and we offer them to other parents in hopes that they, also, will be encouraged. But when we try to turn a proverb like this into a promise, it can become a trite, over-used cliché.

We believe that if we do our part well, then things will go well. What works for one child works for them all. Raise 'em right, they'll turn out right, right? Except that parenting is not a formula with predictable outcomes and guarantees. When children decide to go their own way and deviate from the path we started them on, the misuse of this verse can create guilt and condemnation. As parents we end up thinking any number of blaming, defeating thoughts, such as, *We must not have done a good job "training them up" because our college student refuses to go to church and wants nothing to do with our faith.* Or, we doubt whether we set a good enough example in our homes or read enough Bible stories when the kids were growing up. *The biblical principles we have instilled in our children since they were toddlers don't seem to fit with our culture; we must not have done a good enough job teaching them when they were young.* Some of us hold on to this verse like a magical wish that somehow, someday, all of our children will miraculously come to their senses and fully embrace every spiritual truth we ever taught them. *You know that promise in the Bible, "Train up your child . . . ?" Well I'm holding on to that one for sure!*

A friend of mine graciously gave me permission to share her story of walking a difficult path with her adult daughter.

We tried to raise our daughter up in the way she should go. Of course, we messed up countless times along the way, but I apologized when needed and prayed with her every night before bed. She sat under excellent Bible teaching at church, we read and discussed C.S. Lewis apologetics books together at home, and she had great, genuine Christian friends. We tried to be careful to not push our faith down her throat or act legalistically, and we had a pretty strong relationship with her. So I definitely felt disappointed, heartbroken, and confused when she decided at eighteen years old to leave home, skip college, have nothing more to do with God, and move in with a woman she had fallen in love with.

I had used this verse in Proverbs to falsely and subconsciously convince myself that I could raise her the right way and guarantee her salvation. As a result, I felt a lot of guilt and questioned what we had done wrong. I've had to recognize that I am her mom, but definitely not her Savior. My parenting, good or bad, didn't make her a Christian or cause her to walk away from her faith.

I'm learning to leave her in God's hands and I'm praying that He will open her eyes to see Him as the loving and holy Lord and Savior that He is. Scripture passages about godly kings with sons who rejected God have encouraged me recently. Reading about Samson's praying parents and his escapades into immorality have made me feel less like a failure. And, when I remember that God is the perfect Father and still Israel turned away from Him, I recognize that my daughter has her own will too—and her story isn't over.

Now, I rest in the truth that God is sovereign and good, and I pray for her to seek Him. I notice a freedom in leaving her in His hands, a sigh of relief that I didn't mess it all up, a peace that it is out of my control. As a result, I find that I worry less and I can just enjoy being with her. When she brings up the topic of faith, I am more relaxed while talking to her, and I don't feel the need to change her and convince her of anything. There's less baggage of guilt or resentment, and I can simply love her. I can sincerely pray, "My [her] life is in your hands" (Psalm 31:15).

So how *are* we to read this proverb and others like it? First, the book of Proverbs is a wisdom book filled with sound principles and general truths. We should not underestimate the power of making wise choices and living according to God's Word. Generally speaking, when we follow the principles laid out in Proverbs, life works pretty well. It isn't that life is perfect or that we don't have problems, but rather that overall we enjoy the fruits of living life according to God's design. It's similar in concept to creating a healthy lifestyle. Most people who take care of themselves by eating well and exercising will enjoy healthy bodies and good quality of life. But it is not a guarantee. Some people are genetically predisposed to diseases and medical conditions that cannot be prevented simply from eating well and exercising. Similarly, when we live our lives according to the wisdom of God's Word, we often will reap the benefits of our wise choices. But neither is this a guarantee. All of us can think of godly people we know who have lived exemplary lives and yet have faced all kinds of trials and challenges. And all of us can think of times in our own lives when things haven't gone the way we had hoped, even though we followed the rules.

Furthermore, many scholars hold the view that "train a child in the way he should go" speaks to not only the broad principles of education (physical, intellectual, moral, and spiritual) but also their adaptation to each particular case, in a careful study of individual character and capacity, and with a thoughtful regard to future course of life.[11] In other words, we are to contemplate both the direction and the path we lead our children on as well as *how* we lead them, in keeping with his or her individual gift or natural bent. We need to be students of our children. They are individuals with unique personalities, wiring, and temperaments, and what is effective for one child may not work for another. Children in the same family will often have wildly different personalities and learning styles, and the way a parent connects with her introverted son will most likely be different from the way she connects with her extroverted daughter.

Likewise, when considering spiritual practices and pathways, children have different ways of approaching their faith and connecting with God. One child may love to connect with God through music or art; another may like to listen to stories or read books; still others may feel closest to God when hiking or out on a kayak. Some children seem to absorb everything they learn from a young age and consistently grow in their faith as they get older. It is a steady progression of understanding, growth, and maturity, and their faith sticks. Other children seem to question everything they hear from a young age, and by the time they hit their teen years may be filled with overwhelming doubts about their faith. This can be scary for parents, and it can be difficult to know how hard to push a child to keep going to church or youth group when they clearly no longer want to go.

When our preteens, teens, and college students begin to question their faith and challenge the truths we have raised them up with, it can trigger fear and anxiety for us as parents. We hear young adults talk about going through a "deconstruction" of sorts as they mature—a reassessing of everything they have been taught so they can decide which faith principles they will adhere to as they enter adulthood.

For parents this can feel unsettling, but this process is not necessarily a bad thing. In fact, it is vital for young adults to ask questions and work through their doubts, to seek truth and develop a genuine faith relationship with God. I *want* my daughters to make their faith their own, rather than just carry on our religion the way we carry on family heritage and traditions ("My mom is American, my dad is French-Mexican, we eat pot roast on New Year's Day, and I'm a Christian. . .).

When my eldest daughter was in high school, she went through a difficult season of doubt and struggled greatly with her faith. I worried that, like freshly poured cement, her doubts would harden and become permanent. I mistakenly thought it was my job to talk her out of her doubts, to convince her that all of the things we had taught her about God and Scripture were true. Her strong will pushed hard against mine, until I finally realized I had to give her and her faith journey to God. I had to accept that I was not in charge of her spiritual process.

With two daughters now in college and one in high school, I am finding myself in this interim season where I am trying to figure out how to engage and have conversations about faith and culture when we don't always agree on things. I am clumsily navigating discussions that sometimes don't go very well as I seek to listen and understand, be heard and understood, and continue to guide and come alongside my daughters as they develop their world views and faith perspectives.

In the thick of it all, I am learning some things about my kids and about myself. I am realizing how often my reactions are driven by fear. Through trial and error, I am discovering some important "what to do and what not to do" ways of responding:

1. **Don't freak out.** (I have done my fair share of freaking out.) It can be alarming to hear your child say things or do things that go against what you believe to be true and right.

Often times I over-react. I get emotional. It comes out in frustration—even anger—but under the surface I am scared. I am worried my child may be deceived by false teaching, and on a deeper level, I am scared at the realization that I am not in control.

As parents, we actually have *zero* control. Our children will make their own choices and forge their own faith journeys. We do, however, have *influence*. But our influence will be severely hampered if we are reactive and emotional. Our kids will not feel safe talking to us about their questions and opinions if we interrupt them and do not listen. I have botched many conversations because of my emotional responses, but it is not the end of the world because there is this thing called grace. When I circle back and acknowledge my failure to engage well in a conversation, my child's heart softens. When, in humility, I admit when I'm wrong and acknowledge that I don't have the monopoly on absolute truth or know the answers to all or even most of our hardest questions, defenses come down. And, when I vulnerably admit to my child my fears lurking under my frustrations, I've seen something pretty remarkable happen. She sees my struggle. She sees that I am trying. She sees that *I love her*. By grace, we get to try again. And again, and again.

2. **Don't _not_ freak out**. It's true that we should not freak out (see point #1). But if not freaking out means that we throw our hands up in the air like we just don't care, that we remain silent when we hear things that don't align with our faith and values, that we trust that somehow it will all work out in the end if we give our children all the space in the world to figure things out on their own, then I think we need to freak out *a little*. False teaching should alarm us. Red flags should go up. Like a warning light on the dashboard of our cars, we should pay attention and heed caution. We should pay attention to what our kids are reading and read some of these books ourselves. We should study apologetics and dig into the hard

stuff. It is a huge mistake for us as parents to be silent when our kids need us to be involved. It is neglectful to look the other way when they still need our guidance. Even if they don't agree with what we are saying, I truly believe they *want* connection. There will be times when we need to back off and, for a time, maybe stop discussing certain topics or issues. But we can still engage and be present, both in our actions and by our example. Even as our kids become adults, we can be some of the most influential people in their lives.

Hanging in there, being sensitive to timing and non-verbal cues, and showing respect by how I handle myself in the conversation goes a long way in protecting and preserving the relationship. And this is of utmost importance, because without relationship I have no influence! When I demonstrate that our relationship is more important to me than being right, my daughter's heart towards me softens. She sees that I am not willing to give up or walk away. She sees that because we love each other and are for each other, we keep jumping in. We keep engaging. And in my human, flawed, imperfect way, I will keep trying to be the best mom-mentor I can be.

3. *Do* **trust God.** Trust him deeply, unswervingly, and from the bottom of your heart. And pray for your children. Pray for their friends. Pray for your nieces and nephews because it really is true that God loves these children even more than we do. He cares about the state of their hearts and their faith journeys even more than we do. And, unlike us, he *does* have control over a whole myriad of factors and influences we may not think about. He orchestrates people to cross their paths. He provides a way out of temptation and delivers them from evil. He brings to mind his unchanging truths in precisely the right moments. He uses anyone and anything to do his holy work, and by the work of his Spirit he convicts, reveals, heals, and transforms. Even in our imperfect parenting he uses us—in all our shortcomings—to illustrate and demonstrate the

gospel. He uses our weaknesses to showcase his strength and perfection. He uses our deficits and limitations to show our kids that what they need most can only ever be found in him. By his grace, God redeems, restores, and redirects. As we release our children into his hands, he holds them secure. His love never fails.

4. **Demonstrate biblical dependency and a commitment to live under the authority of Scripture.** This speaks *volumes*. Living the Christian life is not as much about following rules and being a good person as it is about following *the person* who gave His life in exchange for ours. It is about submitting ourselves to the lordship of Jesus Christ, surrendering our lives to his will and good purpose, and placing all of our trust in Him. This means we hold Scripture higher than our own desires and opinions. None of us does this perfectly. By his grace, may we be found faithful.

Our kids must walk their own journeys and make their own choices, and this includes their faith walks. Just like us, they will stumble and make mistakes. Sometimes they make big mistakes and walk far from the path we wanted them to travel. Sometimes the deviations are smaller and less severe, but still not what we desired for our children. If they do wander, grow cynical, or become prodigals and wander far from home, we can stay steady and model a genuine faith. We can pray and keep watching for them to come home. We can walk in humility, acknowledge that we do not have all the answers, love unconditionally, and live in daily dependence on God.

Wise Responders

You will teach them to fly,
but they will not fly your flight.
You will teach them to dream,
but they will not dream your dream.
You will teach them to live,
but they will not live your life.
Nevertheless, in every flight,
in every life, in every dream,
the print of the way you taught
will always remain.

—Mother Teresa

"Help! My child wants to be a vegetarian!" These are the words I typed in the search bar at the library, hoping to find a book that would help me deal with my 12-year-old daughter's decision to give up meat for good.

A couple of months earlier, Claire had begun casually mentioning things like, "Today I ate some chicken at school and then I felt really weird," and, "What if I tried to be a vegetarian for a week, just to see what it's like?" I think she knew I was not going to be enthusiastic about it, so she broached the topic ever so carefully until finally she just refused to eat meat. She said it made her feel sick and she wasn't going to continue to eat it.

I didn't want to force Claire to eat something that was making her feel bad, but I really did *not* want her to become a vegetarian. Some of my friends expressed concerns about Claire being a growing girl and not getting the protein she needed from meat. I was also concerned about her getting the nutrition she needed. And, I was sure this was going to mean more work for me. I love to cook, and Claire has always loved my food. She's the one who would bounce into the kitchen most afternoons asking excitedly, "What's for dinner?" and her favorites included beef stroganoff, pulled pork, BLTs, and chicken parmesan. She was my food buddy.

When I saw that Claire had made up her mind and I couldn't sway her, I decided to get on board and help her learn how to eat healthy without meat. I took Claire for a check-up and had her talk with her pediatrician about the lifestyle change she was making. Not only did he not have a problem with her going meatless, he felt confident that if she learned to eat the right foods, she could develop a very healthy lifestyle. When we left his office Claire asked me, "What are legumes?" We did some reading. One of my vegetarian friends gave us some great tips, such as adding iron-rich spinach to smoothies—you don't even taste it! Claire still wanted to eat fish and shrimp, so I kept individual portions of these proteins in my freezer. They thaw quickly and I could easily adapt what I was making to include these proteins. And, if our dinner didn't work for her, she learned to fix herself a quesadilla or a grilled cheese. As it turned out, my initial fears were unnecessary, and it worked out just fine.

If there is a lesson here, it has to do with how we respond when our kids make decisions that we disagree with or that we don't feel would be best for them. Accepting Claire's decision to become a vegetarian is a cake walk compared to parents who are dealing with their kids' decisions to date or marry someone they don't approve of or choose a lifestyle or path they don't agree with.

When my friend, Ruth, told me about a heart-breaking situation with her son and the way she chose to respond, I remember thinking, *Every parent needs to hear this story*. Ruth and her husband adopted their son from an orphanage outside the U.S. when he was 8 years old and had provided a loving, stable family environment for him and his siblings. Early on, their son struggled with his education and was eventually diagnosed with autism spectrum disorder. Ruth and her husband worked with specialists to try to determine his specific needs and to help him enjoy learning. He had a great high school experience with good friends and very caring teachers, and his family was very proud of him when he graduated. They were unpleasantly surprised when he informed them that he was going to be leaving after graduation and they would probably never see him again. He had decided, after much thought and careful planning, that he was going to ride his bicycle out west and start a new life.

With the help of her counselor, Ruth and her family responded in ways that were counter-intuitive. Her counselor advised, "Don't try to stop him. He's telling you that he wants to be independent, and that is not a bad thing." So Ruth and her family decided to offer help and do whatever they could to prepare him for his departure. Whenever they offered to help him, it caught him off guard because he expected them to try to persuade him to stay. They made a list of things he needed to know: how to make a collect call; how to use the internet in a library; not to let anyone know that he had cash on him; and how to use his medical card. They offered to teach him how to wash his clothes at a laundromat and take care of his basic needs. They told him, "We don't agree with your plans, but we want you to be safe and to be as prepared as possible. Even though you are leaving us, we will never leave you. Your bedroom will always be here for you and you can always come back, no questions asked."

When he did finally leave, carrying a 30 lb. backpack, it was on the hottest day in July with temperatures reaching 107 degrees. His family felt empty. Later that night, he sent each family member (including his three siblings) individual texts. In Ruth's text, he wrote, "I left today, and I came back today.

Twenty-five miles into my ride, God told me this was not his plan for my life." He turned around and went home.

Ruth's story amazes me. My natural inclination would have been to do everything in my power to stop my son from leaving, even if that meant using control and manipulation. And it most likely would have led to disastrous results. A year and a half later, Ruth's son left home again, and this time he did not come back. Although they seldom hear from him, he has a great job and is very self-sufficient and happy with his life. They did all they could to prepare him and make sure he understood that he always has a place in their family.

Ruth's wise response made all the difference in keeping their relationship intact and the door open for her son to come home. Responding with wisdom instead of knee-jerk reactions can have far-reaching effects and a big-picture impact. Sometimes, the thing we most need to do is the exact opposite of what we feel like doing. I'm thankful for people in my life like Ruth, who teach me by their example.

And Now, What?

Grown don't mean nothing to a mother.
A child is a child.
They get bigger, older, but grown?
What's that suppose to mean?
In my heart it don't mean a thing.

—Toni Morrison

As I came out of my bedroom the morning after my eldest daughter, Kate, left for college, I couldn't resist walking down the hallway to her bedroom. I stood in the doorway for a couple of moments looking around her clean, empty room. *She's waking up in Michigan in her new dorm room this morning. I wonder if the foam topper we got her for that flimsy mattress made it any more comfortable?* I headed downstairs to start the coffee, and as I groggily scooped the coffee grounds into the filter, I glanced at the sugar bowl on the counter. *That is the sugar bowl and spoon Kate used every morning to put two teaspoons of sugar in her tea.* I had to remind myself that she hadn't died—she had just gone to college like millions of other kids do every year.

I missed her. After moving Kate into her dorm, the three-hour car ride back to Chicago had been uncomfortably quiet. I was feeling my own sadness and also absorbing the emotions my husband and other two daughters were inevitably feeling about leaving their daughter and older sister behind in another time zone. When I had set the table for supper that evening—our first family dinner as a party of four—the stack of plates was a little lighter, but I felt the weight of one less person seated at the table.

This is harder than I expected. Still half asleep, I poured myself a cup of coffee and splashed in some cream. Then I grabbed a blanket and cozied up on the couch. I needed some quiet time to process what I was feeling. I grabbed my journal, and as I thought about which words to use to express my thoughts and feelings about my baby girl leaving home, a sentence formed in my mind without me even realizing it.

You're fired. Thank you for your years of service, but we need to let you go. I sat there on that couch, coffee mug in hand, startled by the thought. It's amazing what comes to the surface when we get still. There it was—my big fear. For almost nineteen years I had been Kate's mom. I taught her how to talk and walk and tie her shoes. I taught her how to cook and bake. I read her stories and tucked her in and prayed with her before bed. I held her in my arms and on my lap. I held her wrist stable on a board book as we sat in the ER waiting to find out it was indeed broken. I held her after her first break-up, and every single day of her life I have held her in my heart. My fear was that now she no longer needed me.

Letting go is not easy. Those first few months I struggled with my new parenting role. Kate and I texted and FaceTimed a couple times a week, but I tried to let her set the pace. In time, I began to see that she still needed her mom—I just needed to adapt to a new role and adjust to a few job description changes. I had to transition from the director's chair to playing a supportive character in my daughter's story.

When our children are little, we slide into that director's chair quite easily. We aren't exactly given that role, but it fits. We *know* it is where we belong. Even though we are at times plagued by self-doubt, we are absolutely sure there is no one on the planet more qualified than us to run this production. We are, after all, mostly in control—at least of the controllable aspects of our children's lives. We plan their schedules. We choose their bedtimes and bath times, the food they eat and when they eat it, when they can watch T.V., and what shows are appropriate for them to watch. We set limits and boundaries. We select the music they listen to and, early on, the friends they play with. Our influence in their lives—for better or worse—is profound and far-reaching. It helps shape who they become.

As they grow, we begin to loosen the reins and allow them to make some of their own choices. But we may still see ourselves as the screenwriter, director, and producer of their stories. We have strong ideas and opinions about how their narratives play out—which extracurricular activities they should sign up for, who they should or should not hang out with or date, what they should study, where they should work, and where they should go to college. Yet the truth is that, as our children grow, we become much more of a supporting character in their stories whether we realize it or not. Depending on the day, we may mistakenly think we are the creative genius behind who they are becoming or the colossal failure who has messed everything up, but God is the author of their lives. He is writing the screenplay. He is the director—the One who leads and guides their steps. *It has always been him.* He opens and closes doors and allows various experiences to shape their character and faith. He is using us as supportive roles to accomplish his work and his purpose in and through our children, but he alone is the author, director, and producer of their stories. We were never meant to sit in his chair. We were never given that role. It has always been God in that seat, from day one. It just takes some of us a long time to figure it out.

Which brings us back to where we started. As moms, we won't enjoy every moment of this journey, but we can find joy in each season as we walk this road together. Whether our children are boys or girls, biological or adopted, infants or young adults, being a mother of another human being connects us in ways that really matter. We are filled with both wonder and anxiety, deprived of sleep and solitude, stretched beyond what we think we can withstand, brought to tears and to our knees, and overcome with a love so fierce it can only come from one place—the heart of God. Make no mistake: this motherhood gig was totally his idea.

Review:

Letting go is not easy. Our children will make their own choices and forge their own faith journeys, and no matter how hard we try to do our part well, we are not guaranteed a particular outcome. Our attempts to control are like clicking buttons on a remote control with no batteries. We do, however, have *influence*.

Reflect:

1. What would it look like for you to more fully surrender your children and their journeys to God? Are there times you need to get out of God's way so he can do his work in their lives, "letting perseverance finish its work so they may be mature and complete, not lacking anything" (James 1:4)?

2. As your child reaches certain milestones, are you transitioning into any new parenting roles? How are you adjusting to whatever "letting go" looks like in your current season of motherhood?

Respond:

(Enter your child's name in the blanks)
God, thank you that you are the author of _____'s life. You are the one writing _____'s story. Enable me to entrust _____ completely to you, knowing that you love _____ even more than I do. Open and close doors. Lead and guide _____'s steps in your ways and in your truth. Use whatever and whomever you choose to draw _____ to you. Help me to partner with you and not get in your way. Use me to accomplish your purposes, that your will be done in _____'s life. Amen.

Acknowledgments

To my family—Thank you for cheering me on and for your patience during this project. Thank you for allowing me to share some of our stories in the hope that others will be encouraged. Girls, being your mom is a true gift and my life's most important calling. Thank you for your grace as we are all works in progress. And, thank you for asking to write the foreword for this book, believing you were uniquely qualified to do so. Your words are priceless and I love you.

Bernie—Your support of what I do helps me become who God made me to be. Thank you for never asking me, "Why are you doing this again?" And thank you for reminding me—again and again—of the reasons when I ask, "Why am I doing this again?" I love you.

Kate—Thank you for your editorial, creative, technical, and administrative work on this project. Your determination and excellence in all you do is admirable, and I am so proud of who you are. You are a generous soul, an amazing firstborn, an Enneagram 6, and one of my most favorite people in the whole world.

Claire—Thank you for proofing and helping me get the Q-Tips and underwear chapters right. Your wit and humor keep me from taking myself too seriously. Your love for God and others is beautiful. You are an extraordinary middle child, an Enneagram 9, and one of my most favorite people in the whole world.

Brenna—In your younger years, you were affectionately called a spitfire, a handful, a run for our money, and a force to be reckoned with. You are hardworking and tenacious, and watching you live your life with passion is inspiring. You are a spectacular last-born. An Enneagram 3, you are one of my most favorite people in the whole world.

Kari and Margie—If speed dial was still a thing you'd be my first two numbers. I don't even want to imagine doing this journey without you.

To my proofers—Abby, Bernie, Britta, Claire, Kari, Kate, and Margie—Thank you for your time, your honest critique, and for making me a better writer. And to Colleen, Marla, Steph, Tori, and Tricia—thank you for proofing the final draft and helping me cross the finish line!

To my editor, Becky Skillin—Thank you for your excellent attention to detail and your thoughtful developmental sculpting of chapters. What a joy it has been to collaborate with you!

To Beth, Emily, Julie, Rachel, Ruth, Tina, Tricia, and all the other moms who agreed to share their stories in this book— Thank you for being a part of this project.

To Krzysztof Stanczyk—I knew I wanted your photo for the cover of this book the moment I first saw it. Thank you for so graciously allowing me to use it and for sharing your artistic gift.

To Mindy Comincioli—Thank you for creating the book cover of my dreams.

To the Tribe, our small group, and the Chicago Area Speakers Group—You are more than support groups; you are family.

To the Ladies in the Kitchen—Thank you for all the "Mom conversations" over the years. It is a joy to work with such wonderful women.

To all the moms who walk with me, support me, inspire me, and challenge me—Thank you.

To the moms I have connected with over the last decade through MOPS, moms' groups, and through my writing—You are the readers I pictured in my mind as I was writing these chapters. Thank you for sharing this journey with me.

To my Lord and Savior, Jesus—Thank you for your daily guidance, provision, presence, and grace. You alone are worthy.

Notes

1. Oxford English Dictionary, *Lexico.com*, 2020, https://www.lexico.com.
2. John Townsend, *Boundaries with Teens: When to Say Yes, How to Say No* (Zondervan, 2006), 10-11.
3. Amanda MacMillan, "Here's How Many People End Up in the ER Due to Cotton Swabs," Health, May 8, 2017, https://www.health.com/mind-body/cotton-swabs-ear-injuries-emergency-room.
4. Letitia Suk, *100 Need-to-Know Tips for Moms of Tweens and Teens* (Hachette Book Group, 2018).
5. Morbidity and Mortality Weekly Report Press Release, "1 in 3 adults don't get enough sleep," *Centers for Disease Control and Prevention (CDC)*, February 18, 2016, https://www.cdc.gov/media/releases/2016/p0215-enough-sleep.html.
6. Anxiety and Depression Association of America, "Facts & Statistics," *adaa.org*, https://adaa.org/about-adaa/press-room/facts-statistics.
7. Gary Thomas, *Sacred Marriage* (Zondervan, 2015), 51, 266.
8. Joseph Barth, *Ladies Home Journal* (April, 1961).
9. Paul David Tripp, *New Morning Mercies* (Crossway, 2014).
10. Scott Rubin, *The Essential Guide to My New Life With Jesus* (Simply Youth Ministry, 2016).
11. Thomas Thomason Perowne, *The Proverbs* (Forgotten Books, 2017), 142.

Connect with Becky

Dear Reader,

Thank you for reading this book! I'd love to hear how it has encouraged you on your motherhood journey. Let's stay connected! Find me online and subscribe to my monthly newsletter for updates, blog posts, and ongoing engagement around topics of family and faith. If you are looking for a speaker for your next event, you can contact me through my website.

Website:
www.beckybaudouin.com

Facebook:
https://www.facebook.com/Becky.Baudouin.Author.Speaker

Instagram:
https://www.instagram.com/beckybaudouin

May you find joy as you set your heart on pilgrimage, daily find your strength in God, and allow him to shape you through the process of parenting your child.

With gratitude,

Also Available from Becky Baudouin

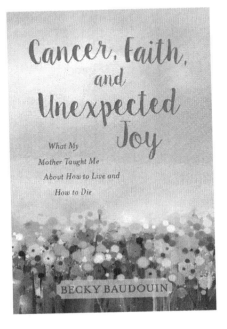

Available at kregel.com and wherever books are sold.

"I've taught you how to live; now I want to teach you how to die. You don't have to be afraid."

For anyone living with the tension of wanting to hold on yet needing to let go, *Cancer, Faith, and Unexpected Joy* demonstrates a powerful and profound love.